JOY
COMES IN THE MORNING

90 DAY DEVOTIONAL

Presented by
Dr. Vernessa Blackwell
and
89 Phenomenal Coauthors

Copyright © 2022 by Vernessa Blackwell.

All rights reserved.

No part of this book may be reproduced in any form or by any electronic or mechanical means, including information storage and retrieval systems, without written permission from the author, except for the use of brief quotations in a book review, magazine, newspaper, website or broadcast.

Scripture quotations, unless otherwise noted, are taken from the King James Version.

Library of Congress Cataloging-in-Publication Data ISBN: 978-0-9601043-6-9

Published in the United States by Dream Kiapers P.O. Box 491, Waldorf, Md 20604

Manufactured in the United States of America

DEDICATION

Lord, Lord...

I am so thankful! It is one thing to know so many great, powerful, enlightening, and successful people. But it is another to be loved back by them. Lord, I thank you. I am bathed in gratitude for the magnificence that surrounds me in this Devotional. I am honestly in awe. Ninety authors, some of the greatest to ever do what they do are part of my tribe, and I am a grateful part of theirs.

And yes, some are famous. World-renowned even. But most aren't. They are giants in my life for simply being who they are in spirit and in the world.

Both professionally and personally, ranging from comrades to authors, from politics to entertainment, business to the arts... I have had the opportunity to sit down with, talk with, and love amazing souls. Thanking God this Joyful morning for the love in my life that keeps me strong and humble every day.

I don't get to speak to you all every day... but just knowing you are there and that we are in this time and space together brings me joy. Some of you I've never met face to face or only a few times. Some of you I've known for over a half-century. You all inspire me, and I know you've made me better as a person.

One coach taught me something years ago when I published my first book. She said, "Vee... when it comes down to it, it's not about who you know, but more about who knows you. Spread Joy wherever you go. Live your life so it makes the world want to be around you and love you."

I must have done that because those of you who have shown up in this book as coauthors blow my mind.

I want you all to know you have blessed me. YOU HAVE HELPED ME TO FIND JOY IN THE MORNING and you continue to do it every day.

So… I want to say I APPRECIATE YOU! I THANK YOU and I LOVE YOU Dr. Vee

Table of Contents

Evangelist Kimberly Babers 1
    The Warrior Within 2
Tanisha Bankston 3
    FROM A CATERPILLAR TO A BUTTERFLY 4
Evangelist Angie BEE 5
    The Joy Found Me! 6
Rachel E. Bills 7
    Joy of the Journey 8
Dr. VernessaBlackwell 9
    When Grief Stole My Joy 10
Alex Bowser 11
    Breathe Human 12
Evangelist Valecia Brimage 13
    My Dad 14
Dr. Lori Butler 15
    When You Meet Grief 16
Ivy Caldwell 17
    There Is Joy After This 18
Dr. Shela M. Cameron 19
    I GOT "JOY" DOWN IN MY SOUL 20
Melodie T. Carr 21
    Restore My Joy, Oh God 22
RhondaBerryhill-Castaneda 23
    INTENTIONALLY JOYFUL LIVING 24
Dr. Khadijah X. Chapman 25
    From Mourning to Self-Made Millionairess! 26

Michelle A. Clark 27
    God Will Do a New Thing 28
Chanelle Coleman 29
    Finding a Rainbow Despite the Gray 30
Juanna CouncilBrown 31
    Value Yourself 32
Dr. Doris H. Dancy 33
    Our Multitude 34
Kymberly L. Davidson 35
    Resilient and Favored 36
D. Suzette Davis 37
    Remembering God When Life Breaks Your Heart 38
Reverend Dr. Patricia A. Johnson Dowtin 39
    Joy Comes in The Morning 40
Alice Edwards 41
    Season of Purpose 42
Kim Evette 43
    Unknown Territory 44
Marilyn Fenderson 45
    He Keeps Me 46
Dr. January Few 47
    Ordered Steps 48
Darkema Freeman 49
    IN THE MORNING 50
Matice Freeman 51
    TALK TO GOD 52
Sakinah N. Freeman 53
    Reflections of a Conqueror 54
Deborah Juniper-Frye 55
    Coping Through the Unexpected "Seeing Your Glass as Half Full" 56

Joey Gadah ... 57
Running the Right Race ... 58
Dima Hendricks ... 59
Lessons Through the Pain ... 60
Apostle Patricia A. Henry ... 61
Been There, Conquered That ... 62
Elsie D. Hepburn ... 63
CHILDREN ARE A BLESSING, SERVE THE LORD WITH GLADNESS! ... 64
Erica Yvette ... 65
Little Brother ... 66
Tekesha Hicks ... 67
Praising During the Struggle ... 68
Paula Hollis ... 69
J.O.Y. The Ongoing Destination in The Grief Process ... 70
Dr. Angela Hood ... 71
Look Again to Live Again ... 72
Dr. Renee Huffman ... 73
Wait On The Voice Of God ... 74
Dr. Maisha Jack ... 75
RELIEF, SOOTHE, BREEZES, And DEFENSE ... 76
Sandra Jackson ... 77
All of Heaven Is on Your Side… Rejoice! ... 78
Dr. April Johnson ... 79
The Miraculous Exchange ... 80
Rowena Jones ... 81
Favor the Widows ... 82
Candy J ... 83
Peace Be Still ... 84
Theresa Jordan ... 85
God Has Done Great Work in Me, and He Is the Author and Finisher of My Faith ... 86

Cheryl Kehl 87
   Created to Win 88
Marnie Lacy 89
   Daddy's Girl 90
Karen Lewis 91
   When God Interrupts Your Life 92
Dr. Tina D. Lewis 93
   It's Not Funny! 94
Dr. Maribel Lopez 95
   Hope 96
Dr. Fikisha Marée 97
   Happy Desert Blues 98
Brandee Martin 99
   Healing "Daddy Issues" 100
Dr. Celeste Johnson-Matheson 101
   Finding Joy In Your Brokenness 102
Dr. Y'LondaMitchell 103
   Grief to Gratitude 104
Bethzali Mongare 105
   I Am Restored Piece By Piece Daily 106
Bianca Moore 107
   Stop Interfering in God's Business 108
Dr. Barbara J. Neely 109
   The Two Faces of Grief 110
Dr. Thomasina "Denice" Nicholas 111
   The Press That Leads To The Oil Of Gladness" 112
Shywanna Nock 113
   Don't Stop, Don't Quit 114
Dr. Adrienne Reed Oliver 115
   The Art of Letting Go 116

Issata Oluwadare **117**
    The God Who Sees Me 118
Sheena Vendoria Parson **119**
    Amen'd 120
Leona D. G. Partis **121**
    Post-Traumatic Stress Disorder 122
T.K. Peoples **123**
    Repossessions to God's Double Blessings! 124
Troy Rawlings **125**
    "Night Cries & Sunlight" 126
Debra Riddlespriger **127**
    Restore And Reset 128
LaTonya Kirksey-Roberts **129**
    Keep Pushing 130
Malissa T. Roberts **131**
    When Joy and Mourning Walk Hand in Hand 132
Ronnette Rock **133**
    Then Comes Resilience 134
Dr. Radiance Laveena-Nicole Rose **135**
    Faith On Fire 136
LaTia N. S. Russell **137**
    The Day My Father Died… 138
Dr. Angela Seay **139**
    Pressing Forward, Keep Moving "Procrastination is NOT your friend!" Dr. A. Seay 140
Rev. StarshaSewell **141**
    Five Faith-Based Strategies to Overcome Loss Onset by Injustice 142
Elaine EzzellShelley **143**
    Love - Trust - Believe 144
Loretha Simon **145**
    Though I Mourn Their Passing, Just Thinking of Them Gives Me Joy, Which Comes from
    The Lord 146

Darlene Smith 147
    Cheffin with Joy 148

Takia Chase-Smith 149
    Joy During Trials 150

Valerie Stancill 151
    Just Joy 152

Rosa Sylvester 153
    The Power of Thankfulness 154

Winona L. Thomas 155
    Refined for Resilience 156

Shaunda Thompson 157
    Bent Not Broken 158

Erica D. Tobias 159
    Seasons Change 160

Shanta' Tobias 161
    There Is Still Purpose to Fulfill 162

Tamron Tobias 163
    I Am God's Thoughts 164

Arlene Townsend 165
    Your Joy Is Coming 166

Ray'Chel Wilson 167
    A DEVOTIONAL FOR DADDY'S GIRLS 168

Verlisa Wearing 169
    Arise and Shine 170

Dr. Jenaya White 171
    The Promise of Restoration 172

Stephanie White 173
    Clouds …Faith …Decisions 174

Malcolm Winder 175
    Forgiving What You Can't Forget 176

Dr. Angela Basden-Williams 177
    Keep Shining Bright Like a Diamond 178
Yonder 179
    Who Am I? Why Am I Here? 180

Evangelist Kimberly Babers

is an educator, published author, and a retired United States Army Service Member. She believes in the empowerment of people through the Word of God, Kingdom living, and the power of prayer. Connect with her on Facebook, Kimberly Babers.

The Warrior Within

"Many are the afflictions of the righteous: but the Lord delivereth him out of them all."
(Psalm 34:19)

Looking back over my life there have been many adversities and difficult times. Adversity comes in many shapes and forms, unexpected hindrances, disappointments, roadblocks, and setbacks which God often used to test my faith. Many challenges and adversities resulted from overcoming a broken marriage and raising my children alone with little support from family members while in the military.

The hardships of constant duty assignment relocations and separations from my family during my military service put a stain on my children's stability especially during the times I spent away from home. During those times of adversity, I relied on the never-changing hand of the Lord, The Lord has always been my source of strength and joy.

The year was 2005 in Baghdad, Iraq when my faith was once again tested and tried. Being a single parent and a leader of soldiers in the combat zone pushed me to be mentally tough; I was smack dab in the war zone for the third time. Once again, I was in harm's way. At this point in my military career, 17 years of my life were dedicated to serving and protecting my country from all enemies foreign and domestic.

Only the strong will survive, persevere, and endure to the end despite the circumstances. Survival depended on my ability to be mentally and physically tough. 'I will never give up even in the face of adversity' one motto I live by. In weakness, I am strong with God on my side. God's mercy, grace, compassion, and faithfulness gave me hope to endure many hindrances, disappointments, and adversities. I thank God for helping me push past my adversities and make out of the war zone.

Tanisha Bankston

is a single mother of three children. She is a survivor of rape, incest, childhood sexual abuse, trauma, and domestic violence. My purpose is to help other people, especially women and children. It's time to get unstuck and move forward! My website is www.mypainismypower.com and my Facebook, Instagram, LinkedIn, Twitter is all Tanisha Bankston

FROM A CATERPILLAR TO A BUTTERFLY

"I can do all things through Christ who strengthens me."
(Philippians 4:13)

My name is Tanisha Bankston. I am a single mother of three children. I am a survivor of rape, incest, childhood sexual abuse, trauma, and domestic violence. My abuse began when I was between the ages of five and six years old. When my family left, a man forced himself on top of me, pulling my legs open and forcing himself inside of me. I cried. I was screaming. I kicked him off me.

I got up and ran across the railroad tracks crying to my mother saying to her, "a man just touched me down there." My mom instantly called the ambulance. I was taken to the hospital. My siblings and I were later taken by DHS and placed with our family members.

I thought I would be protected and safe. The abuse continued. One of my male cousins would come into my room late at night and have sex with me and put my foot against his penis until he masturbated. I was manipulated to have sex with one of my aunt's boyfriends at 10 years old.

The grandson of the neighborhood candy store owner manipulated me to have sex again at 11 years old. At age 13, my cousin's husband got me pregnant, and I became a teen mom at 14. Still, at 14, a guy on Church Street manipulated me to have sex with him and I entered a Domestic Violence Relationship with him from the age of 14 to age 23. I've been in abusive and dysfunctional relationships to where I was beaten and left for dead. My favorite scripture is "I can do all things through Christ who strengthens me." (Philippians 4:13)

Evangelist Angie BEE

serves the Lord with gladness as an ordained ministry, motivational speaker, and entrepreneur. Angie BEE has been recognized as an International Amazon #1 Best- Selling Author through her contributions to several anthologies. She writes a monthly column in the national Triumphant Magazine and leads a virtual writing workshop!

Visit www.DaQueenBee.com
Follow www.Facebook.com/AngieBEEproductions

The Joy Found Me!

"Do not be anxious about anything. Instead, in every situation, through prayer and petition with thanks giving, tell your requests to God. And the peace of God that surpasses all understanding will guard your hearts and minds[a] in Christ Jesus." Philippians (4:6-7 NIV)

How did I find joy after loss? Which story would people want to read about, Finding love after divorce or living with hair loss? I went to Facebook and asked my followers what THEY want to read about. The votes came in, and now, I will share with you my hair loss journey.

I was diagnosed with Alopecia Areata in my mid 20's. I wore wigs and hairpieces until my 50s. My daddy helped me learn how to shave the patches of hair from my head and try to accept a bald head; there is no cure for this auto-immune disease that destroys the hair that my body grows. I was still covered with wigs because I was doing the work of an Evangelist, and the "church" told me I had to be covered. It wasn't until God sent Bartee to find me that "The Joy in The Morning" chased me down!

During our first date, I thought I would scare Bartee away by revealing my bald head. I didn't want to submit to another man due to the pain I felt from abuse and abandonment. When I removed my false eyelashes, wiped away the eyebrow pencil, and snatched off my wig, I thought he would say "Good-Bye." Instead, he said, "You look like a China-Baby" and he smiled. His joy chased me down!

After we married, Bartee always accompanied me to go out in public without my wig. Then, we were encouraged to launch a fashion show featuring ALL BALD MODELS! Now, our annual philanthropic event invites Alopecian's to be Bold, Beautiful & Bald - TOGETHER! The joy I feel each September has chased me down! Allow joy to seek you out and elevate you - even with a bald, shiny dome!

Rachel E. Bills

is the owner of Women of Virtue Publishing Company and she has published 9 anthologies. Through the company, she has helped dozens of writers become first-time Authors and has provided a platform for both writers and authors to build their brands. She is always looking for individuals who desire and are ready to share their stories and influence with the world.

For Rachel's Books www.rachelebills.com
Follow on Facebook and IG: @ rachelebills Women of Virtue Publishing
(916) 407-4055
rlandbills@wovpublishingco.com

Joy of the Journey

"For God hath not given us the spirit of fear; but of power, and love, and a sound mind." (2 Timothy 1:7)

While recently conversing with my 22-year-old daughter, Dajanae, I asked her what she thought about the words in this title. Her response was, "Finding happiness in the process." Makes sense.

I still remember how it felt not knowing what my purpose was in life or if I was even close to discovering it. I was a young mother and the thought of me not accomplishing anything or making something of myself in front of my children was unbearable. I wondered about my gifts, what my testimony would be, and more so, how I of all people could affect others. Then life happened.

I experienced so much sorrow and betrayal I no longer even looked for the signs of my destiny. I felt defeated. But thank you, Jesus, God never gives up on us.

God showed me first, that He had been there the whole time. Every time I sat up crying all night, couldn't eat, couldn't sleep, and during days of total dread, He was there! I wanted to quit school because of my pain but got the strength to keep pressing. I almost lost my mind but felt the love in me and didn't. I didn't know which direction or way to turn when my husband left me, but I felt a sense of clarity that led me. All the time God was there!

Whether pain caused by others or illness caused by a pandemic, I can now say I have joy in the journey. And I no longer walk in fear, but in victory, because I know He is there.

Dr. Vernessa Blackwell

is an Award-winning author and Certified Grief and Joy Restoration Coach. Losing both parents and all her siblings, including three sisters and a brother, sparked her purposeful journey into coaching. Vernessa is the author of The Grief Helpline. And she is a mentor, Visionary for this project, and International Speaker.

WHEN GRIEF STOLE MY JOY

"For his anger endureth but a moment; in his favor is life: weeping may endure for a night, but joy cometh in the morning." (Psalms 30:5)

The scripture "*weeping may tarry for the night, but joy comes with the morning.*" Psalms 30:5; may have little meaning to someone amid grief. When someone is grief-stricken, sad, and hopeless, the road ahead may appear dark, long, and very lonely. But joy, it will come!

A phone call came in that Paul, my Love for over 30 years, would not be coming home. He had been involved in a car accident and did not survive the accident. Life at that moment for me would forever be changed. Grief stepped right in and stole my joy. Days turned into months and months into years, and the grief continued to overcome me. Year three was approaching, and I started an online coaching support and connection with other women. The first six months, the group felt like home, a place of solace and rest. As time moved on, I felt something stirring on the inside of me that wanted more than to connect online. I wanted to do more to support others stuck in grief. At that moment, I felt hopeful about the future.

One morning during my journaling time, I started to journal ways to help women move towards joy. The feeling of excitement, hope, and joy overcame me, and three hours later, I had an entire plan to start the Grief Helpline to support others and help them restore Joy.

One Year Later, I launched the Grief Helpline, and helping others became my passion. Although joy did not come after one night of sorrow and grief, it did come, and my joy was restored. Discover more @www.griefhelpline.coach

Alex Bowser

Born in Denver, Colorado, Alexander has had brushes with death, drug addiction, and depression and has since forged his pain into triumph. He now leads Sales teams that crossed over the million- dollar mark, achieved the title of Certified Executive Life Coach, produces music, and writes books spanning three genres.
His debut self-development book entitled, Breathe Human - Dancing with Devils, is centralized around his life's tragedies and the path he has forged in pursuing his life's calling.

Breathe Human

"But if we walk in the light, as he is in the light, we have fellowship with one another, and the blood of Jesus, his Son, purifies us from all sin." (1 John 1:7 NIV)

When a child is firstborn, the first act every soul walking this earth first takes in is their Breath of Life. It is a beautiful moment when life is brought into this world as a blessing from God. This blessing was you. When you came through into this world, you were looked at with beauty and love by a higher power, blessed with a power that resides deep within and only you can bring it forth into this reality.

Throughout our lives we are often tested and tried, burnt, and destroyed. This is often the case in which we allow ourselves to fall back and recede from our gifts, shying away from being vulnerable and stepping forth into the light. However, these tragedies are our muse. Should you view them as blessings in disguise and push forward unto them, you will step up on the mantle of greatness and shed a radiant light unto all those who you meet along your journey, but only if you choose.

We have deep within us a great primordial power we call, "Willpower". This is a divine right given to us that when acted upon, has afforded mankind the ability to do many great and terrible things. This is also your power. After diving deeper into the pit of my hell, with drugs, depression… torment, and despair, I had ripped my life apart and floated out of alignment with my purpose. Out of alignment with my gifts. This is how I know the road you are on is difficult. It is blurry, muddy, and bloody, but that does not mean you can give up.

You, my dear friend, you beautiful soul, have a light within. This is the same light of the divine sovereign that birthed you. You never know who, what or when you will influence greatness by not giving up, but rater fighting back towards the Light.

Evangelist Valecia Brimage

has always known that God created her to do amazing things in His name following her father's footsteps. Guided by the Holy Spirit, Brimage wrote, self-published, and completed her first two books in the years 2016 and 2018. She is also co-author of several book anthologies.

Social Media:
Facebook – Author Valecia Brimage Facebook – Free2worshipministries
Instagram – Author_ Valecia _ Brimage Instagram – Free2worshipministries
Website Info: www.valeciasbooks.com

My Dad

"Therefore, my beloved brethren, be ye steadfast, unmovable, always abounding in the work of the Lord, forasmuch as ye know that your labor is not in vain in the Lord."
(1 Corinthians 15:58)

Loving and caring toward others with a sincere heart to see souls saved is how I describe my Father. In October 2000, my world shattered into a million pieces at the passing of my beloved dad who not only was a true man of God but was well-known for helping others in the community. He would give the shirt off his back. The very food he would be eating he would go without to satisfy a starving soul.

It was hard accepting he would no longer be here with us. The thought of living without him bothered me intensely as his absence ran through my mind daily. My dad was the backbone of our family. He was the glue that held us together. How do I move on without him? Some days were unbearable, but when I thought about the good times, those times helped me get through.

Being followers of Christ, we learn as believers, our works do follow and we should work out our soul salvation. The joy I found was in knowing that the legacy he left behind, I have done what most of our fore fathers desire, and that is to pick up and carry the baton handed over to generations to come.

You may be grieving the loss of a loved one, I encourage you to look deep within the memories of those that have gone on before you and continue to carry the torch of hope. That is how I found my place of comfort and closure. I close with the words of Apostle Paul in 1 Corinthians 15:58. *"Be ye steadfast, unmovable, always abounding in the work of the Lord, for as much as ye know that your labor is not in vain in the Lord."*

Dr. Lori Butler

is a mother of two beautiful teenagers, one of each. Lori is a Texas native. Best Selling Author, former Educator, Business consultant, Insurance litigation consultant. Lori is active in the disability community. Lori received master's degrees, in health, and business administration.
Lori's Doctorate is in business. God always sustains her endeavors.

When You Meet Grief

"For no one is cast off by the Lord forever. Though he brings grief, he will show compassion, so great is his unfailing love. For he does not willingly bring affliction or grief to anyone". (Lamentations 3:31-33 NIV)

Each one of us will meet grief in our lives. The question remains which type of grief will present itself. Most people consider the worst grief as losing a child, as it is unnatural for a parent to outlive a child. Others consider the loss of a spouse devasting, and they often die of a broken heart.

There are levels of grief denial, anger, bargaining, depression, and acceptance (Kubler & Kessler, 2022). I never associated grief with pregnancy, but it happened. Here I was excited, barely showing, a new mother who could hardly wait, with doctor appointments that had absolutely no concerns.

I prepared for a December arrival, but one night early in October I felt horrible. I drove myself to a hospital to discover my blood pressure was near stroke level. Pregnancy-induced blood pressure is called preeclampsia. I was 27 weeks.

Long story short, My OB care flighted me to his hospital. I had quick emergency surgery, and my daughter weighed one pound. I was in intensive care for two weeks. My daughter was in NICU for seventy-two days, with health issues from premature birth. Ultimately, I left the hospital without my daughter. I had lost both parents, several close friends, and experienced intense levels of grief. However, this grief was different as there was no involvement, participation, or normalcy. As a new parent, the traditional transition into parenthood had been stripped away from me. It is okay to grieve. God's word is never void. Joy comes in the morning always.

Ivy Caldwell

is the Founder of the "Stepping into ANEW You" Coaching Program which is faith-based and serves those who are ready to confront their emotional trauma and move forward to be healed. She is an ordained elder, certified Christian counselor and life coach, wife, mother, grandmother, 3X's author, course creator, speaker. She is the author of "Expose It" where she shares her testimony of being an overcomer. Her website is: https://footprintenterprisesllc.com
Podcast: Stepping into ANEW You
You can follow her on the following social media platforms:
Facebook and YouTube: Ivy Caldwell Instagram@footprintseries

There Is Joy After This

"But don't just listen to God's word. You must do what it says. Otherwise, you are only fooling yourselves. For if you listen to the word and don't obey, it is like glancing at your face in a mirror. You see yourself, walk away, and forget what you look like." (James 1:22-24 NLT)

We all face those tests, trials, challenges, downfalls, life- altering experiences, the unbelievable situations in our lives. Then we have those "I didn't see it coming" moments. What are we to do when life happens? We are to get up, dust ourselves off and keep it moving. Wash your face, put on some makeup, and dress yourself up even when you don't feel like it. After you do this, you still feel like crawling back under the covers, with the shades closed and you turn your phone off. You don't want to be bothered and you don't want to talk to anyone. You have to face whatever it is and deal with it.

Honey, it's okay to feel what you are feeling, but what you can't do is stay there. It's okay to cry, shout it out and write it out. Grab a notebook or journal and write how you feel and be honest with yourself. If you don't have anyone that you trust to talk to, begin a conversation with God today. Whatever you need to say to God, He can handle it.

"Cast your burden on the Lord, And He shall sustain you; He shall never permit the righteous to be moved." Psalm 55:22

In time you will look back and thank God for that experience. You are stronger and wiser because of it. God so amazes that He will use our weakest and lowest moments for our good. *"And we know that all things work together for good to those who love God, to those who are the called according to His purpose."* Romans 8:28 God will use everything we go through for His glory! In time, God will restore your Joy to you after this.

Dr. Shela M. Cameron

is a spiritual and dedicated leader committed to the community (locally and abroad). She mentors, teaches, builds relationships and businesses, educates, provides resources, knowledge, and networks to promote opportunities for people. She enjoys traveling, and meeting people, and loves the Lord. For information go to https://savvyauthorshela.mystrikingly.com

I GOT "JOY" DOWN IN MY SOUL
"Weeping may endure for a night but JOY comes in the morning." (Psalm 30:5)

What is JOY and why is it important? JOY is internal and sustainable happiness that is a soul-rooted sense of well- being at peace with yourself and with the world around you and not in pieces. JOY is important because it opens up ways to feel passion, inspiration, imagination, and creativity to a greater sense of fulfillment in our lives. It also boosts our immune systems, fights stress, and, pain, and improves our chance of living a longer and healthier life. I've had many weeping nights, but joy came in the morning. My relationship with God is the key to peace. Cultivating JOY is essential to happiness. My recommendations to accomplish and obtain JOY are:

- Give yourself permission to be Happy and then aim for JOY
- Never forget that you deserve happiness.
- Ask yourself the right questions – What can I do to ensure a Joyful state of mind?
- Make JOY your daily intention – Embody and carry with you the way you want to feel with higher vibrations.
- Ensure your home is a haven of peace, calm, and JOY – Give yourself a daily time-out for Soul-Care
- Do things that open you up to JOY – talk to GOD, pray, read a book (The Bible), chat with a friend, have new adventures, travel, inspire others, be creative by writing, journaling, painting, gardening, cooking, etc.
- Connect with nature – Listen to Alexa sleep or nature music
- the ocean or rain. It is so peaceful and calm. Also, outdoor walks and mediation. All of this will automatically reduce stress and anxiety.
- Last but not least, THANK GOD AND PRAISE HIM EVERY DAY because weeping may endure for a night but JOY comes in the morning!!!

Melodie T. Carr

is a mighty praying Woman of God, who through Jesus Christ, has been forgiven, made new, and restored in God's abundance; US Army; US Veteran; Disabled Veteran; SiStar; Sigma Phi Psi, Soror S.T.O.R.M.

Connect with her @ MTCAgency@outlook.com.

Restore My Joy, Oh God

Did you lose your joy? Do you want your joy back? God's sweet, beautiful, soul saving joy! That spiritual unspeakable joy! Well, did you pray for it?! Go ahead, ask for it, I dare you, pray for it:

Restore my joy, Oh God, in the holy name of Jesus, Amen!

God takes brokenness, puts it back together again, and makes it better than it was before as God's promised to us is a better way, a better life, and a better future. To renew your spiritual joy is to submit, surrender and recommit to God:

"Create in me a clean heart, O God; and renew a right spirit within me!"

The same applies to restoring the Joy of God's salvation. Simply ask God for it, pray for it:

"Jesus Christ, my redeemer, and healer come into my heart, Oh Lord, become my savior, Oh Lord! God, the beginning and the end, the alpha and omega and the most powerful God in heaven, on earth and under the sea. Oh God, I humbly come to you in prayer for the restoration of the joy of your salvation, Oh God, I come in prayer for all your heavenly and spiritual fruits of goodness and blessings, and lastly, Oh God, I'm praying for you to restore all your gifts of joy, Oh God, way deep down in my soul, in the holy names, blood and spirit of Jesus Christ, Amen! Amen! Amen!"

Restoration Is Always in Abundance

Biblically, restoration is always in abundance when something is restored; it is always better than what it was, to begin with. God not only restores you; He restores you in abundance. **Remember, you must also ask God for it, in prayer through the name of Jesus Christ.**

Rhonda Berryhill-Castaneda

is a married mother of three children from Southern California. She holds a BA in Child Development, is a Childhood Educator, Child Life Coach, Children's Book Author, Co-Author, and Owner of Cherished Child Coworking Preschool.

INTENTIONALLY JOYFUL LIVING

"IN EVERY WAY AND EVERYWHERE WE ACCEPT THIS WITH ALL GRATITUDE." Acts 24:3

How do we find joy in the morning? What is intentionally joyful living? It is claiming our joy and taking it back! After experiencing deep loss, we must reacquire our right to be joyful and participate in happiness. Whether your loss was professionally, romantically, physically, or death, the grief is deep sorrow. It is a practice of being joyful once again.

There are numerous ways to live joyfully, but the most important and first step is to exercise the art of gratitude daily. Finding joy in the morning may not come naturally after a profound loss. However, it is during the mourning period where it is imperative to express gratitude. We must feel grateful. We need to be filled with gratitude because God gave us another day to enjoy life on earth. Let us rejoice in the love we found. We ought to be thankful for the physical body that is strong and able to house our soul. It is essential to be grateful for family members still with us. We should be pleased to have friends surrounding us with love and know we are an integral part of their stories. Give genuine thankfulness that God trusted us to parent our children. We shall show appreciation for the knowledge we possess to be employable. Let us give thanks and praise for the years we spent with our family members and friends who have passed on and cherish the memories we made together. The joyful, loving moments shared will never be erased. It was real and we are eternally grateful for that time together. Thanks be to God.

We cannot control unhappy, inevitable circumstances which we encounter in our lives. However, we can manage our behavior with our gratitude. Through our gratefulness, we will once again master the art and find joy in the morning.

Dr. Khadijah X. Chapman

Coach Millionista-
7 figure Strategist- Self-Made Millionairess– Founder of The Black Millions Matrix
Dynamic-Speaker, Author, Visionary, Millionaire Maker I'm Committed to Your R.A.D.I.C.A.L Success
MY PASSION IS BEING a 7 FIGURE Strategist.
My Mission is Your Way Too Millions
I created the "ichoosemillions.com" MOVEMENT to impact millions into creating MILLIONS.

From Mourning to Self-Made Millionairess!

"Everyone also to whom God has given wealth and possessions and power to enjoy them, and to accept his lot and rejoice in his toil—this is the gift of God."
(Ecclesiastes 5:19 ESV)

I went from being abandoned (by mom) to living swell (with dad, his sister, and GMA) to being a struggling parent on welfare to being a felon to engineering multi-millions 27years self-employed, Accredited investor Self-made millionairess first million achieved in 9 months, most recent million accomplished in 4 months (during the plan-demic). While helping entrepreneurs add 5 and 6 figures to their bottom line.... And it's been a maze of despair, doubt, and ultimately wonderment...

However, because of my past, I became fearless, creative, abundance-driven, non-negotiable, and unapologetic about my mission to engineer black millionaires while being RADICAL.

My mantra...'*You find success in life relative to the areas you're willing to get "radical" about! And in my world "RADICAL" is. Results Achieved Daily Intentionally Creates Amazing Living.*'

My passion is helping entrepreneurs discover their "Radical" Factor. So, they CAN create their "Radical" Rise ($1 Million within a year). Creating 7 figure strategies is SIMPLER THAN YOU THINK. We don't have money problems. We have wisdom challenges. My life's journey has shown me that getting RADICAL-Results is key to winning, and who you team up with will sharpen you or land you on a couch watching someone else's movie. As Coach Millionista I create 7 figure strategies that'll allow you to pay for, direct and star in your movie! Money is an equalizer. My Net Worth is $4 million.

Michelle A. Clark

*Attended Bennett Career Institute for Make-Up Artistry.
She's been a Make-Up Artist since 2009. She's participated in the following: New York Full Figure Fashion Week, Maryland Fashion Week, Ms. Black America, Ms. Africa USA Pageant. Published work is seen in Encore HD Hair Magazine. Michelle has been an Ordained Elder since 2011.*

God Will Do a New Thing

"Forget the former things do not dwell on the past. See, I am doing a new thing! Now it springs up; do you not perceive it? I am making a way in the wilderness."
(Isaiah 43:18-19 NIV)

I never thought in a million years it would come to a point of being my Mother's Caretaker. My mother Carolyn was a vibrant, lively woman with a sharp sense of humor. As an only child, I watched my mother die gradually. It was a disheartening situation to watch daily. I prayed often, I wanted her to live, but God was ready for her to live with him.

Trust God when you can't trace him was becoming a tangible mindset every day I watch my mother. God, I miss her. I wish she was still here. She is about to be a great- grandmother in July. I just want one last hug, another Watergate cake, more fried potatoes, another hard laugh.

Trust God, you say…I trust God through every tear I cried, I leaned not to my understanding and gave it to him. The new thing God has done for me is a new level of mental peace despite what I can't understand.

The resounding question I ask myself is "Would my mother want me to stay depressed?" The answer is no. She clarified it on her sickbed. She wants me to live for God and live without regrets. Create the business, make sure her granddaughters excel and the last thing she told me was to allow no one to take advantage of me! God is doing a new thing: A new mindset, A dimension of Purpose, A dimension of Prosperity, and a new dimension of Peace.

Chanelle Coleman

is a native of Milwaukee, Wisconsin. She is the creative powerhouse behind CeCi's Ink, an innovative storytelling company that conveys powerful narratives through poetry, books, playwrights, fashion, blogs, and motivational speaking. She is inspired by her late mother's penchant for prolific storytelling and developing a strong sense of faith.

As a survivor of abuse, Coleman believes in the communication skills she developed to cope in those environments. She is also an accomplished playwright Please check her website for details. Her greatest accomplishment, however, forever remains becoming mother to her six beautiful children and "Gigi" to her two grandchildren.

Finding a Rainbow Despite the Gray

The morning began like any other. I remember lying in bed not wanting to get up, exhausted from running my household. Thankfully today I could relax; my aunt was taking care of my 16-year-old, Taniyah. For six years she'd been living with the effects of anoxic brain injuries, today she would have an attentive caregiver instead of the zombie I felt I was turning into.

Suddenly a frantic call tore through my moment of solitude. I walked into the room and found Taniyah unresponsive. Words can't aptly describe seeing a void in the eyes that once held so much excitement and luster for life. My family fought to hold onto her, desperately praying for a miracle. I stood there anxiously waiting for God to perform it. But the emergency response team who took over our efforts pronounced my angel dead.

Her death, however, was not an acceptable answer. How could this be part of His will? I wanted to know why. For six years I had managed a state best described as happy hurt but now I was asked to grapple with this.

Was I angry, hurt, and discouraged? Yes! Without a community of loved ones interceding with God on my behalf, I would not have survived. My world instantly turned gray, but God guided in bits of color to show me He was still watching over me.

I've learned that difficult moments help to produce gratefulness for every blessing. If you're in a dark season, create a gratitude journal. Jot down the bits of color that jump out from the gray. Write down the answers to even your smallest prayers, they aren't prayed in vain. Find someone to cover you in prayer. Beloved , Christ promises the blessed hope of a resurrection. No more pain, death, or mourning, only unspeakable joy!

Juanna Council Brown

*Hello everyone, my name is Juanna Council Brown
I live in Blythewood, South Carolina. My social media is @juanna.council (IG)
Juanna Council (Favebook0
YouTube Channel is Jcouncil1996. My email is juannab48@gmail.com. Twitter
and LinkedIn are Juanna Brown. I want to inspire others to believe in
themselves.
And we all will WIN!!*

Value Yourself

This brings me to a quote I was thinking of: "*You may have cried today. But guess what. We are human, we were gifted with feelings. Value yourself*"! Despite all the tears I've cried all the heartbreak from friends and relationships, doesn't disqualify me from being a valued person. What disqualifies us as a human, is how we think of ourselves and how we handle different situations.

So again, don't let society disqualify us from being great. I sat down with myself and said why am I letting what others think of me slow me down on what I want to accomplish. That's when I realized I had been blessed the whole time, but due to my struggles and my feelings, it was blinding me of my blessings. I prayed and I asked God to strengthen me so I wouldn't feel low. I asked God to strengthen my mind so I could be in a positive place. I prayed and asked God for peace within my mind. Just know with God we can accomplish everything we put our minds to.

Never forget we have the strength to keep going, but we also must realize we need God in our corner. I learned to humble myself in all situations. I needed to be more grateful and appreciate what I already have. I must be me and never change unless I see the change will benefit me. I must always rely on me, and avoid thinking that having others in my life will make me happy. God and I will make me happy.

Dr. Doris H. Dancy

is an award-winning educator, speaker, writing consultant, novelist, and editor. She is the writer of the award-winning Redemptive Love Series: Jagged Edges, Shattered Pieces, and All Other Ground. In December 2021, she published a poetry and micro-fiction book entitled And the Word Became Flesh. www.dorishdancy.com

Our Multitude

"Taking the five loaves and the two fish and looking up to heaven, he gave thanks and broke them. Then he gave them to the disciples to distribute to the people."
(NIV)

In Virginia, on January 3, 2022, some areas experienced snow flurries, others dusting on the grass, while others, on Highway I95, felt the wrath of the storm. Travelers sat in the cold all night. They were hungry, thirsty, cold, and lacked restroom facilities. They tried to keep warm with whatever they could find, but all seemed hopeless.

Remember, however, God always shows up in a storm. There was a truck filled with bread also stuck. The driver realized his vehicle could not move, so he carried loaves of bread to the long line of hungry travelers. God had sent a miracle.

Sometimes, it's natural to assume the problems facing us are too difficult to handle; this is how the disciples felt when they faced their hungry multitude; however, we must realize we are never alone. God will multiply our small portion to a degree it can help many. This man could have said there was not enough bread for everyone; he could have thought it too difficult to walk to so many individual cars. Instead of excuses, however, he did what he could, and God supplied the rest.

While our light is always too dim, the Lord adds the increase. When He gives us a gift, an idea, or an opportunity, He keeps His promise never to leave or forsake us; therefore, we must never hesitate to let our light shine. Never fail to believe that what God puts in our hands will multiply in His. This man was in that truck, on that highway, with those loaves of bread. It was all a part of God's divine plan: to consistently demonstrate He is available to meet our needs regardless of the difficulties we face.

Kymberly L. Davidson

is a proud HBCU graduate and holds double Master's degrees. Kymberly is a domestic violence advocate and a survivor of both domestic violence and cancer at the same time. Kymberly is a published author with new works soon to be released. Kymberly is the CEO and Founder of Arise Mpowered, LLC. She is the mother of two adult daughters and has two grandchildren.

Resilient and Favored

Trials and tribulations have been abundant to many of us. We have been thrown into a season of uncertainty due to the effects of the COVID-19 pandemic; including imposed isolation, the shutdown of businesses and schools, and lack of fellowship with friends and family.

It is a lot to cope with. To make matters worse, as we slowly are released from the grip of the pandemic, we are now bombarded with the suffering and devastation of war around the world. I want to offer some consolation and encouragement. No matter how hard it gets, there is always tomorrow.

Hope for a new beginning; a new opportunity.

1 Peter: (NKJV) says, *"And after you have suffered a little while, the God of grace, who has called you to his eternal glory in*

Christ, will Himself restore, confirm, strengthen, and establish you?" You have the ability and the faith to stand firm; resilient.

Ephesians 6:11 (NKJV) says, *"Therefore, put on the full armor of God so you will stand firm against the devil's adversities."*

We have all heard the encouraging words, "delayed but not denied" (citation unknown). Many references in the Bible confirm that the promise can be greater despite a delay.

Consider the story of the inflicted woman and Jairus' daughter. In Mark 5:25-42, Jesus is called to the bedside of a dying girl. He is delayed by the bleeding woman who touched his garment in faith of being healed of her chronic ailment. In his delay, two miracles happened. The woman was healed, and the child was brought back to life. But God! So, remember whose you are, despite troubles you face. The comeback will be greater. Be encouraged, be resilient, and have faith. You are favored.

D. Suzette Davis

is a nurturer by nature, enthusiastic about motivating people to be the best version of themselves. She is an accomplished Equal Employment Opportunity Professional, talented author, and exceptional real estate agent. Above all, being a devoted mother and grandmother has brought her the most fulfillment.

Remembering God When Life Breaks Your Heart

A widow's journey, at the very least, can be exceptionally tumultuous, with multiple unforeseen highs and lows and twists and turns. Overall, it's an emotional rollercoaster that seems to have no end. Finding joy in the morning, afternoon, or night can be a formidable and inconceivable task. When the unimaginable happens in your life, there's an overwhelming feeling of helplessness that renders you powerless.

It can feel as if you cannot fathom you have the strength to take your next breath, while simultaneously you question if that breath is even worth it.

While you are stuck debating the most basic human function, breathing, the world and people around you go on with life as usual. While you are desperate for time to stand still, every part of you struggles to make sense of what has happened and to see a life going forward.

You may feel broken, but you are not defeated and it's okay to not be okay. With each sunrise, God allows us to live our best life, even if it doesn't resemble the life we had.

I imagine no matter where you may be in this world, the amazing beauty of a sunrise is undeniably majestic and gives the assurance that God hasn't forgotten you and his love is unwavering. God promises, joy will come in the morning. Although it may be several mornings later, in time, joy returns.

I encourage you to do simple and positive things that bring you joy daily, I find joy in walking and listening to music. And last, be kind and speak positively to yourself. Over time, this will bring you back to believing in the endless possibilities God has for you. Remember, YOU are worth fighting for, always!

Praying for an abundance of peace and love.

Reverend Dr. Patricia A. Johnson Dowtin

*Born & raised in Washington DC Married the late Joseph T. Dowtin, Jr.
mother of Monique Morton, Unique Dowtin, and grandmother of
Joshua Morton
"If I can help somebody as I travel along, then my living shall not be in vain."
email: 1pa.johnsondowtin@gmail.com*

Joy Comes in The Morning

We see in The Message (MSG) Bible as recorded in the (Book of Psalms 30:1-5) A Psalm of David. A song at the dedication of the temple.1 I give you all the credit, GOD—

[YOU] got me out of that mess, you didn't let my foes gloat.

2-3 GOD, my [GOD], I yelled for help, and you put me together. GOD, you pulled me out of the grave, gave me another chance at life when I was down-and-out.

4-5 All you saints! Sing your hearts out to GOD! Thank [HIM] to [HIS] face!

He gets angry sometimes, but across a lifetime there is only love. The nights of crying your eyes out give way to days of laughter.

In the King James Version (KJV) of the Bible, Verse 5 teaches us:5 For [HIS] anger [endures] but a moment; in [HIS] [favor] is life: weeping may endure for a night, [but joy cometh in the morning].

I have learned there is only one way, only one genuine way "JOY SHALL COME IN THE MORNING" - it shall only come in having a relationship with GOD! Your relationship shall be with the TRIUNE GODHEAD. Other names may be the HOLY TRINITY of the BLESSED TRINITY, yet the name means the UNION OF THREE PERSONS, the FATHER, the SON, and HOLY SPIRIT in one GODHEAD.

Yes, "a RELATIONSHIP where two or more concepts, objects, or people are connected, or the state of being connected.

- the state of being connected by blood or marriage.
- an emotional and sexual association between two people.

Spending quality time with HIM reading your BIBLE, PRAYING, LISTENING to HIM, and PLEASING HIM is all a part of bonding and having JOY…in the MORNING!

Alice Edwards

is a Carolina girl living in a global world, and a professional Children's Librarian who encourages and inspires others to walk in their greatness. Follow me on my Facebook and Instagram social media platforms as me, and subscribe to my Words of Wisdom [tell your story] YouTube channel.

Season of Purpose

"And we know that for those who love God all things work together for good, for those who are called according to his purpose." (Romans 8:28 NIV)

God can speak to us in so many ways. He is the creator of everything. He gives perfect gifts to all creation. As the seasons change, every living thing is affected and prepares its way for its next level. Walking out my front door, I rescued the most beautiful American Dagger caterpillar looking for a place to belong- to transform into its divine purpose.

They are a bright yellow with black spikes and are poisonous. Do not pick them up. With time, this living creation spun a cocoon from a leaf to a tree branch around itself to hide for an extended period. It will grow into an American Dagger Moth- a big, fierce, nighttime warrior.

This message was delivered right to my door. It reminded me to stay strong in moments of change. You are on purpose. And, your life has meaning. Our experiences in life, become our words of wisdom. In the broken places you find your purpose.

Over time, we will all grow in wisdom, and mature in purpose as we experience life on so many levels. Open your ears. Open your eyes. And open your heart. Learn to see and hear God in all living things everywhere you go!

It is time to transition- Change is here! Tell yourself -This is not where I will be forever.' Find your purpose. Reach for your goals. Walk in your gift. And, you know what? Purpose will pop through. Just a Word of Wisdom.

Kim Evette

is a two-time author committed to writing stories about empowerment, motivation, and spirituality. She holds an undergrad in Human Services and a master's in behavioral psychology
Social Media: Kim Simmons -FB @kkeve123
Tiktok Kimsimmons51

Unknown Territory

One of my fondest and most life-changing memories of my adolescence is My Mother introducing me to Jesus Christ. As a family, we attended church and my mother played an intricate part in my spiritual life. My mother was a devout born-again Christian, and there are so many other vivid memories which include heart wrenching, loving, and humorous days.

I heard the word dementia in my early twenties, not knowing the severity and how deteriorating this disease is. I remember watching a Lifetime movie many years ago that depicted every aspect of this illness. I was unaware it would be the fate of my mother and me in several years to come. The movie played out in real life, and unfortunately, it wasn't scripted. Dementia became evident in our lives. Small things began to happen like losing keys, forgetting overdue bills, and forgetting phone numbers. This became a daily occurrence. The latter stages went from forgetting family to becoming bedridden. Galatians 5:22 -23 KJV the fruits of the spirit became my daily mantra, the fruits being, love, patience, and long-suffering.

The Joy came in those fleeting lucid moments when life was simple again and My Mom was her old self.

Marilyn Fenderson

is a Pastor, Bestselling Author, Christian Counselor, Prayer Intercessor, and Kingdom Builder. She has authored ten books.
Pastor Marilyn is the founder of Marilyn Fenderson Ministries and along with her husband and ministry partner she is the co-founder of their marriage ministry One Flesh Worldwide Ministries
www.marilynfendersonministries.com

He Keeps Me

"Cast your cares on the Lord and he will sustain you; he will never let the righteous be shaken." (Psalms 55:22 NIV)

One morning as I embarked on my daily walk, I reflected on the goodness of God and how far He had brought me since my mother's death. My mother was my best friend, confidant, and cheerleader. When I lost her, it felt as though I had lost a piece of my soul. I fell into a deep depression; I didn't want to interact with people or engage in any activities. I laid in bed for days saturating in my sorrow.

Being a pastor, I am trained in grief counseling and assisting others with working through loss and the associated pain. With all of my training, I still couldn't conceive why her death had crippled me so terribly. One day, I had an epiphany, and I heard the Lord's voice say, "cast your cares on me and I will sustain you." I wasn't willing to hear those words because I wanted to keep grappling with my grief. Nevertheless, those prophetic words started my healing process, so I trusted the Lord and stood on his promise.

In difficult times, cast your burdens on the Lord because His arms are big enough to carry them. Allow Him to be a buffer when the enemy plays tricks on your mind. Allow Him to be your strength in times of weakness. Allow Him to undergird you when you're unable to stand firmly on your own.

When the cards and well wishes stop and the phone calls and text messages cease, the Lord keeps you. When the visitors and family leave, He stays. Joy now comes in the morning and I've found peace through my strength in God. As I endure letting go, He keeps me.

Dr. January Few

is a school psychologist and licensed professional counselor by profession. January holds a Doctoral degree in Counseling Psychology. She is a published author of Pretty Introspection, a workbook for women focusing on reflection.

For more information contact her at Januaryfew06@gmail.com.

Ordered Steps

"Direct my footsteps according to your word; let no sin rule over me." (Psalm 119:133)

If you believe that your steps are ordered, then you know that every obstacle you encounter in life has a purpose. Your life is purposeful. The experiences you have whether good or bad are lessons meant to carry you from one area of growth to the next. They act as steppingstones, lifting you to higher ground.

Sometimes you will stumble and fall, but your bruises and scars are meant for you to remember what you have come through. Ordered steps. There are no accidents, no meaningless lessons nor encounters with people, because your steps are ordered. God has a plan for your life even when you have no idea what His plan may be.

Too often in life, I have chosen one path, and God has rerouted and said that is **not** the path for you. I have been denied, disappointed, and disgruntled but have still come through renewed and refocused.

Ordered steps. You may be questioning, God why me? Why does my life seem to spiral out of control? Why do I seem to get into the same mess repeatedly? Why are others thriving and I am still barely surviving? **Ordered steps.** Your mess is a message! Turn your spiral into being spiritual. Reset your relationship with God and remember you are never alone. God will not forsake you, because you have **ordered steps.**

Say this affirmation when feeling down. My God is with me, and I will get through.

My life is purposeful. My future is greater.

My steps have been ordered.

Darkema Freeman

is the mother of four, Grandmother of 1, 3X Bestselling Author. Her passion and hobbies are cooking and crafting.

IN THE MORNING

Psalm 5:2-3 (NIV): Hear my cry for help, my King, and my God, for to you I pray. In the morning, Lord, you hear my voice; in the morning I lay my requests before you and wait expectantly.

Psalm 30:5 (NIV): For his anger lasts only a moment, but his favor lasts a lifetime; weeping may stay for the night but rejoicing comes in the morning.

Lamentations 3:22-24 (NIV): Because of the Lord's great love we are not consumed, for his compassions never fail. They are new every morning; great is your faithfulness. I say to myself, "The Lord is my portion; therefore, I will wait for him."

Sometimes there is something special about the quiet solitude of the sun rising. There is something so spiritual it can catch you off-guard, and make you take a moment and take in ABBA Father. Each new day is precisely planned for you to be reminded of His love and care. ABBA Father's compassion fails not. It is our comfort and satisfaction to hope and quietly wait for the salvation of the Lord.

ABBA Father, a new day is here, filled with hope, filled with You. I earnestly searched for You today in this parched and weary place in my life. Let me see You and Gaze on Your power and glory. Draw me into intimacy with You by Your Spirit to experience Your loving-kindness. May I proclaim with the psalmist that your unfailing love is better than life itself? How I praise You. I will honor You if I live, lifting my hands to You in prayer. Thank You, for Your promise those who seek You will find You. Amen

Matice Freeman

is a Customer Service Representative in Washington DC. She is single, loving and free spirited.

TALK TO GOD

Psalm 34:18 (CEV): The Lord is there to rescue all who are discouraged and have given up hope.

Proverbs 17:22 (NIV): A cheerful heart is a good medicine, but a crushed spirit dries up the bones.

Isaiah 57:15 (CEV): Our Holy God lives forever in the highest heavens, and this is what he says: Though I live high above in the holy place, I am here to help those who are humble and depend only on me.

Are you feeling down? Talk to ABBA Father. He hears. Be honest about your feelings. You don't need to pretend that you're fine when life hurts. When in distress, it is the constant practice of believers to cry unto ABBA Father. It's okay to cry. Be sad. Mourn. Grieve. Ask Abba Father to help you believe that tomorrow will be better. The righteous are taken under the special protection of the Lord.

ABBA Father, I want to know, see, and experience You in fresh ways so I can truly say that I desire You more than anything on earth. You and You alone are the strength of my heart. You are all that I need, and I am so thankful that You are mine forever. Nothing can separate me from Your love. Open my eyes and grant me a fresh vision to constantly see Your beauty, and Your love for me. I know you rescue those with crushed spirits. Wrap Your loving arms around me and heal my broken heart. Amen.

Sakinah N. Freeman

is a Licensed Social Worker, Psychotherapist, Certified Grief Counselor, Licensed Insurance Agent and Author. Sakinah is the Founder and Owner of Healing Hearts, Mind and Soul LLC, which provides, Psychotherapy, Life Insurance and Grief & Loss Counseling.
Website: <u>healingheartsmindandsoul.org</u>
Email:info@healingheartsmindandsoul.org

Reflections of a Conqueror

The worse suffrage of mankind is the death of a loved one. The immense pain, guilt, and anger begins to transient through your body and soul. You desperately want this pain and sorrow to end. The summer of 2021, I would endure this pain, after losing three loved ones, while I was battling COVID. This is my testimony:

I was angry with GOD. The word is "Teach my hands to war." Every night I prayed to my heavenly father to keep me and my family safe, but my prayers went unanswered. I guess GOD went on a sabbatical and forgot to leave someone in charge because Satan was busy and determined to make me his next victim.

One day, I heard my sister's voice in my dreams, telling me to "Get Up and fight"! You're a conqueror and can't be defeated. Your kids and our family need you. I was battling COVID for over 30 days. I was tired! I had no energy to fight but with all my strength. I listened and followed my sister's voice. "All you have to do is "Get Up."

And so, I rise. My life changed instantaneously. I found new meaning and purpose in my life. I am still here! I am grateful for the time I had with my loved ones. I am honored to keep their memories alive and share pieces of them with the world. Through my loved one's gifts, strengths and aspirations came the birth of "Healing Hearts, Mind and Soul LLC. I help the bereaved through their grievance process and assist families with planning their homegoing services.

God's strength is limitless, and GOD will not give us more than we can handle. After your loss is the gain. We die to grow again. There is treasure in every tragedy. "Conqueror".

Deborah Juniper-Frye

Grief Care Consulting, Owner; Grief Recovery Method Specialist; 23 Years of Grief Experience and Expertise; Life & Recovery Coach; Amazon Best Selling Author 4X's; Global Conference Speaker, and a Contributing Writer for OWN IT Magazine.

My website is www.griefcareconsulting.com email address is dfrye.gcc@gmail.com.
- *Instagram @griefcareconsulting*
- *Facebook @ DeborahFrye*
- *Twitter @GriefCConsult*
- *LinkedIn @ DeborahFrye*

Coping Through the Unexpected "Seeing Your Glass as Half Full"

"Consider it pure joy, my brothers and sisters, whenever you face trials of many kinds" (James 1-2)

When I think of the unexpected (unforeseen, unanticipated, or sudden), my thoughts are almost endless. The hardship of loving and losing is a part of being human, and when we lose someone or something, we have deep sadness and grief. It could be the death of a loved one, dealing with self-shame, a divorce, hardship, trauma, or a terminal illness. Life has a way of disrupting our peace and there may be a season when you feel like you will not make it. I've learned that the unexpected can be dealt with in a few ways ~ your attitude, acceptance, or being determined to use it as a learning tool of progress. The bottom line is, we will all face these challenges, and the quickest thing to do is to "see your glass as half full, instead of half-empty.

The phenomenal thing about dealing with the unexpected is that no one has to do it alone. Through this difficult journey, we must find our H.O.T. (However, Over Time) Spot. However, Over Time, this too shall pass; However, Over Time, you will find renewed joy; However, Over Time, God will see you through. God can carry you through any situation and bring you out on the other side with peace and hope. Joy Comes in the Morning is a great reminder that the Lord is waiting for you to seek Him. He can overflow you with unspeakable joy and peace that surpasses all understanding, no matter how stressed and worried you are. Be intentional to see your glass as half full and be a witness that God's Grace is sufficient. He wants to help you find your joy in the morning.

Joey Gadah

is God's warrior by choice. Engineer by trait. Wellness Entrepreneur by passion. Business Owner by family legacy. Uncle by God's blessing. Author/Life Coach by purpose on purpose.
You can find me on social media by searching Joey Gadah or @joeygadah

Running the Right Race

"So, the last shall be first, and the first last: for many be called, but few chosen."
(Matthew 20:16)

We often celebrate the praises, but don't think about the preparation and process of becoming great. We salute ourselves because of our accomplishments but don't think about the hardships we had to overcome. We love the trophies, but we can only imagine the trials. I think we all can agree, that to rise to our level of greatness, we need focus, discipline, and unwavering faith to be the master of our skill.

Greatest Of All Time (G.O.A.T.) status for me is getting up every day being the conqueror of my mornings and running the right race. Running the right race will look different for everyone. We want to be first, we want to be the best, and we want to be different. But we often magnify the what and the how while we minimize and diminish the why because we go after the achievements and accolades while we ignore the applauses and approvals. It is often said comparison is the thief of joy, and unwavering faith is needed in these moments, the "Flex Your Faith Muscle" (FYFM). This faith muscle will allow us not to take things personally when running our race but rather focus on blocking out all the noise from others and not playing the comparison game.

To achieve this level of being great, you have to be committed to wholeness, because it all starts with the foundation…You have to know your definition and motive as it relates to achieving greatness. You have to have an "endzone mindset" and a whatever it takes kind of grit mentality to achieve this greatness. Your greatness will be unique to you and only you, and that will be rare, and rare is never supposed to be crowded.

Now…Go Run Your Right Race!

Dima Hendricks

Sickle Cell Warrior, she is a Sickle Cell Health Coach and the writer of "Unleashing Royalty: A R.O.Y.A.L Formula to Help You Walk into Queendom with Purpose." She is also the host of the #ThroughThePain Podcast. Learn more about Dima by visiting, www.DimaHendricks.com.

Lessons Through the Pain

"Though the Lord gave you adversity for food and suffering for drink, He will still be with you to teach you. You will see your teacher with your own eyes. Your ears will hear him. Right behind you, a voice will say, "This is the way you should go," whether to the right or the left." (Isaiah 30:20-21 NLT)

I was born with sickle cell anemia and experienced painful crises as early as six months of age. As time progressed, I developed a toxic relationship with the inherited blood disorder. During my most excruciating bouts of pain, I repeat the following statement: "If the sickle cell was a person, I would whoop their..." (insert colorful expletive here.) Although sickle cell is one of my most cunning adversaries, it is also the catalyst that leads me to God's wisdom. Here are the two most important lessons I learned through the pain.

Lesson 1: Pain Refines

Pain is a tool God uses to refine and mold you into His image. During your most difficult encounter, you may feel as though you are trapped in a fiery inferno. This overwhelming ordeal is the time you are at the height of your refinement process.

Lesson 2: God is in Control

Pain is the brain's alarm signal. When you experience pain regularly, pain programs you to think that you are in distress or danger. In my desperation of trying to avoid pain, I participated in an experimental stem cell study. Unfortunately, the study did a number on my body and almost killed me. In retrospect, I now realize this thorn in my flesh is molding me for God's purpose. I may not trust my body, but I can trust God. He holds my life in his hands. There is no way to avoid pain. You can't walk away from it, you can't walk around it, you must go through it. Here are questions to consider: In what ways are you avoiding pain? Have you considered if your interventions are blocking God's plan for your life? Do you trust God through the pain?

Apostle Patricia A. Henry

a woman of great courage and faith and the Establishmentarian of The Trees of Righteousness Deliverance Ministry and My Solomon's Porch Ministry. She has an immense passion and exemplifies humility and grace as she is led by the Holy Spirit.

Been There, Conquered That

"Nay, in all these things we are more than conquerors through Him that loved us." (Romans 8:37)

It was the thought of being in basic training that caused me to realize all that I had endured was a precursor to where I am now. Back when I was in basic training, we had to exercise our abilities on the "obstacle course". An obstacle is defined as a series of challenging physical obstacles that an individual, team, or animal must navigate, usually while being timed.

When going through the obstacle course it started to be easy but the more advanced the course was, the more effort was required, not because they were difficult, but because it was a lot of physical and mental energy dispensed. I never took much thought into how challenging it was until the Lord caused me to reflect on my experience. I was being prepared for battle.

The scripture tells us that "we are more than conquerors through Him that loved us". The word "conquer" is defined as to gain or acquire by force of arms; to gain mastery over or use great effort. This love that the Lord has for us is not only comforting, but it is protective, provisional, and especially inseparable. We learn by reading the chapter we are "more than conquerors" because we have been given victory over any and every situation, trial, or test. We are HIS. Our ability to conquer goes far beyond our human abilities.

The Bible tells us in Philippians 4:13 *"I can do all things through Christ who strengthens me."* Celebrate the victory, with your hands raised, with radical praise, or with a shout! You are more than a conqueror! Be Encouraged!

Elsie D. Hepburn

originally from the Bahamas, now resides in South Florida. As an RN / Midwife, health has been her primary focus. After many years in the Medical Field, she transitioned into the Financial Services Industry. Ministry involvements include Youth Camp and Vacation Bible School.

Website:
https://wsbcampaign.com/elsiehepburn/workshops.com
Email: ps23tlc@yahoo.com

CHILDREN ARE A BLESSING, SERVE THE LORD WITH GLADNESS!

"Children are a gift from the Lord; they are a reward from him are like arrows in a warrior's hands. How joyful is the man whose quiver is full of them!" (Psalm 127:3 NLT)

It is summer, time for Vacation Bible School (VBS). Always an exciting opportunity to engage boys and girls in Bible stories, songs and choruses, Bible verses, games, and arts and crafts. Initially, it is difficult to predict how many children will attend. Will we have enough supplies and Teachers? How well will the team games play out? There are the loud and rambunctious, the timid, the "pick me, pick me," and the "I don't want to play."

A rhythm of exciting then quiet songs and choruses get us off to a great start. There is Bible story time, and Bible verses, followed by quizzes. Next, various outdoor games. Team competition rages, tempers flare …Phew!!! Back to order, and calm with arts and crafts. Begin preparing for the closing program for parents and guests. Keep them safe, active, and learning while having a super fun-filled VBS. A tall order!!!

What are you making? Oh, I see a beautiful collage. Glue stuck stuff together and colors ran into a unique work of art. There's fierce competition between teams. How will they accept the final scores? What excitement! Boys and girls are eager to show what they have learned and accomplished in the few days of Vacation Bible School, giving prizes and the closing program.

WOW, not always the picture of calm, and serenity…boys and girls everywhere. Activities off track, where did the time go? Exhausted! Will the numbers continue to grow daily? Do we want more laughing, jumping, excited little ones? Will we make a difference, will every child hear, and take away something immortal? He promised that His word will not return void. No question, it is worth it all! Yes, joy comes in the morning of service!!!

Erica Yvette

is a published author blessed with the spiritual gift of encouragement. She loves being available to give a word of advice, hope, and encouragement or just being an ear to listen.

Connect with her on Facebook Erica Yvette and at ericayvette.com.

Little Brother

"You turned my wailing into dancing;
you removed my sackcloth and clothed me with joy."
(Psalm 30:11 NIV)

was six years old when mom brought home my new baby brother. I'm officially a big sister. I always felt responsible for him and tried my hardest to protect him. He didn't like that. He felt as though I was trying to be his second mother. As he got older, he made bad choices that resulted in serious consequences, and I couldn't protect him. Because of some of his life decisions, I was afraid for his safety . . .Always praying for his safe return whenever he left home.

January 14, 2006, my worst nightmare came true. Someone had taken him from me. My little brother was killed. The morning he died, I remember feeling guilty for not crying. His life had been so full of turmoil I felt a sense of relief. He was no longer suffering from his addiction and no longer consumed with the darkness of this cruel world.

How do you heal when someone takes your loved one away? How do you heal when no one knows why, when no one comes forward and when no one is held responsible? You pray! Not just for yourself but for the person who caused this pain. Holding grudges and anger keeps you stuck in that pain, forgiveness is a must! Although we may not have received justice for him, I know that God knows all and sees all.

God has been so faithful in easing the pain of losing my only sibling. I asked God to give me peace and he did.

So much has happened in my life I wish he was here to see, but I am grateful for the time we had and the memories I have of him. I carry with me his sense of humor, his smile, and his sweet spirit.

Rest on little brother.

Tekesha Hicks

is a licensed Minister at Restoration Church of Daytona. She loves the Lord and has operated in a prophetic dance ministry for over thirteen years. God has allowed her to share that gift with other ministries and that brings her joy. Tekesha obtained a Bachelor of Arts in educational studies with a minor in psychology from Bethune Cookman University. She furthered her education in 2020, at which time she earned a Diploma of Practical Theology from International Seminary, Daytona Beach Satellite Campus. Tekesha has been an early childhood teacher for seventeen years. Looking forward to the future she was recently led to pursue other avenues. She enjoys traveling and reading African American Christian Books.

PRAISING DURING THE STRUGGLE
(Psalms 30 NIV)

Reacting to hurtful events can make us saturated with anger, bitterness, fear, worry, and loneliness, especially if we have felt the pain of a loss, a position, or a thing. God knows each hurt, he not only knows, but he cares for us. Not only does God care but he can restore us by filling us to change our pain. God needs us to trust him with our different situations. God wants us to hand over our burdens to him and we will find immediate peace while we are in the same circumstances. While we are waiting for things to change, we should sing praises and dance like David.

Prayer:

Lord, I give my mourning and sadness to you. Please turn them into dancing and gladness. May I put forth my wailing to you, so you can transform it to dancing and joy? In Jesus' Name.

Paula Hollis

is an Author, Transformational Speaker, Life Coach, and Project Manager who uses practical wisdom and a systems approach to resolve complex life problems. She will encourage, inspire, motivate, and hold you accountable to your goals and assist you in developing a sensible action plan to achieve them.

www.paulahollis.com

J.O.Y. THE ONGOING DESTINATION IN THE GRIEF PROCESS

"Therefore if any man is in Christ, he is a new creature: old things are passed away; behold, all things become new."
(2 Corinthians 5:17)

Finding joy after grief is an ongoing process. I've experienced such grief and loss, from my brother when I was 15 to my sister and husband, most recently around Thanksgiving 2021. A common thread has emerged through each loss. Life must strategically continue for those who remain. While my strategy matures, I focus on the destination of J.O.Y. in the journey. Allow me to explain.

is the destination of Jesus or Christ, the anchoring component of overcoming grief. 2 Corinthians 5:17 KJV states, "if any man is in Christ, he is a new creature: old things are passed away and behold, all things become new." You are found in Christ as you understand and apply his written Word, producing life more abundantly in you. Personal grief is affected because things are seen from the perspective of Christ. His thoughts are not our thoughts, so becoming more like Him changes our thought life.

O is for openness, an accommodating attitude receptive to new ideas. Life changes dramatically in grief as new skills and responsibilities become necessary. An openness toward those changes allows for a much smoother transition and implementation. The new creature in Jesus must now have new ideas rooted in faith, courage, and belief.

Y is for yourself. Through the grief process, you will discover more about yourself as you reflect on memories of your loved one and as you learn your own boundaries and triggers. As these are examined, his Word provides wisdom and instruction to overcome them and introduces even more self-awareness. Jesus, openness, and yourself are the reciprocating processes of overcoming grief and finding J.O.Y. in the journey.

Dr. Angela Hood

A native of Eden, NC, this walking, talking change expert is ordained, and the owner of Alafayeh Candles, LLC. Angela is the founder and host of The One Word Morning Show on Facebook live and on television in Charlotte, NC, Atlanta, GA, and more.

www.theonewordmorningshow.org

Look Again to Live Again

"What do you want me to do for you? Lord, I want to see," he replied. Jesus said to him, "Receive your sight; your faith has healed you." (Luke 18: 41-42 NIV)

Molested at 5. Pregnant at 16. Married at 19. Divorced at 23. Married again only to divorce again. My brother dies in a car accident and my dad dies from cancer. Embarrassment, failure, shock, and disappointment seemed to be my life and lead to my depression. I didn't want to live. If you have encountered many setbacks and have lost sight of yourself and who God says you are, I have an encouraging word for you…Look again so you can live again!

God is asking you, "What do you want me to do for you?" It's okay to ask Him to allow you to see what He sees concerning you. God wants you to live. He wants the best for you. You must understand that existing isn't enough. You must live. There is so much for you to see and you can't quit before you see it.

I encourage you to reconsider your situation and see that God is working it out for your good. This man received his sight because of his faith. He saw what he could never see before. You must have enough faith to stand against the enemy and see what you have never seen before. Maybe you couldn't see peace, love, victory, or deliverance. Problems are not the end of you. There's a solution and I am grateful that the chaotic things that occur in our lives don't have to take our lives. Do yourself a favor and look again, so you can live again.

Dr. Renee Huffman

Publisher of Women of Dignity Media focuses on telling the stories of incredible women impacting their local, national, and global communities.
FB Renee Huffman

FB Business Page: Women of Dignity Media IG:DressedNDignity

WAIT ON THE VOICE OF GOD

"Let me hear in the morning of your steadfast love, for in you I trust. Make me know the way I should go, for to you I lift up my soul." (Psalm 143:8)

I want to encourage you today to wait on the timing of God. This passage of scripture demonstrates the forbearing the individual displays while waiting for God to answer. These persons rejoice in their waiting instead of being disappointed or discouraged.

I remember being a young follower of Jesus Christ, and I changed my closet into a prayer room. I would pray and wait for hours to hear the audible voice of God for his directions and to connect but it did not happen right away, I had to trust God to answer and learn how to wait on God.

God was teaching me how to wait and to know in my heart He already answered my request, and the answer was yes. To receive God's answer, we must be very patient because the answer is coming from eternity and the word of God teaches us to look at things first in the natural then spiritual. When we think of time, we refer to the natural and when we refer to the spirit it is eternal time. God has answered your request, but your answer is based on time, and it takes time to catch up with an eternal God.

I leave you with a prayer. Prayer Point:

Dear Heavenly Father, I will patiently wait on your answer for my life knowing you are working behind the scenes on my behalf. I will continue to wait because I know the outcome is eternity.

Dr. Maisha Jack

Ed.S., is a child of God. Being an educator and leader for the past 24 years in the states of Kentucky and Georgia, Maisha is also a wife, mother of 3, business owner, author, co-author, and recently penned an Amazon Best Selling Author. Visit maishajack.com for more information.

RELIEF, SOOTHE, BREEZES, AND DEFENSE

"For I know the plans I have for you," declares the LORD, "plans to prosper you and not to harm you, plans to give you hope and a future." (Jeremiah 29:11 NIV)

Have you ever looked at a package of HALLS cough drops? Unbeknownst there were four types: RELIEF, SOOTHE, BREEZES, and DEFENSE. Also on the package was the verbiage, "The right HALLS for the right moment." I thought to myself how those words define what God is and has been in my life: The right GOD, for the right moment. Hallelujah!

With the world experiencing COVID-19, quarantines, and all the subsequent variants, my desire for God to become a stronger force within me and my life, has greatly increased. I desire and need RELIEF from racing thoughts in my mind. I desire for God to SOOTHE my heart and pray for the Holy Spirit to BREEZE into my life's situations. I seek progress for spiritual and earthly healing quickly and easily while knowing that everything good, is not always easy. I thank the Lord Jesus for being a DEFENSE all around me and my family because the enemy knows my praise and faith pleases God.

HALLS may relieve the throat and cool nasal passages, but I am grateful to God, who relieves, soothes, breezes, and defends ALL passages in my body and my life. When the world is in chaos, when my core beliefs are challenged, and when the enemy tries to set up camp within my household, a mere package of cough drops reminds me of 2 Timothy 1:7 KJV- **"For God hath not given us the spirit of fear; but of power, and love, and a sound mind."**

Sandra Jackson

is an evangelist, published author, Podcaster, life insurance agent, mother of nine, Radio and TV Host, and more. Contact her via the website at sandrarumph.com or her YouTube channel at Evangelist Sandra E. Rumph-Jackson.

ALL OF HEAVEN IS ON YOUR SIDE… REJOICE!
"And he brought forth his people with joy, and his chosen with gladness" (Psalm 105:43)

Today is your day to become acquainted with the joy of the Lord. Trouble may show up as if it's your soulmate. Don't fear. God has intentionally blocked trouble, and it can no longer locate you. Isn't that good news? Joy will overtake you when you take your eyes off of your circumstances and focus on God's word. In Psalm, God used Moses to deliver the Children of Israel from Egypt. Immediately, they rejoiced and sang songs of Zion. They were familiar with hardship, living under harsh circumstances for years, and hadn't made it to the Promised Land.

However, Moses was appointed as their deliverer. They faced exile and captivity, yet they persevered. Can you imagine, your day of deliverance showing up at your front door? I can imagine you dancing and praising God? They didn't return with sorrow; they replaced the spirit of heaviness with buoyant joy. If hardship, no longer existed, what would you offer God in return? God delivered me from cancer, divorce, and kept me from the evil that lurks in the shadows. I must rejoice. As the Children of Israel praised God, He rewarded and promised them sorrow and sighing would no longer be their lot (Isaiah 51:11).

A feeling of happiness comes from Jesus alone. The Holy Spirit brings joy. Natural joy occurs when a person gets hired at a Forbes 500 company or births a baby. Achieving the unachievable causes temporary exuberant emotions because joy is a choice. When feelings of defeat arise, release unconventional Joy. God stands with outstretched arms waiting for your surrender. He wants you to know that all of heaven is on your side. When the enemy attacks your faith, rejoice! Had not God stepped in on time things would have been different. David received the Ark of the Covenant back He danced with all of his might. Your joy level depicts the depth of your breakthrough. All of heaven is vouching for YOU

Dr. April Johnson

is a Multi-Business Entrepreneur, International & National Public Speaker, Pastor, Youth Advocate, Philanthropist, and Author of inspirational, devotional, domestic violence, poetry, and children's books. She resides in Florida with her husband, Min. Samuel Johnson. She has 4 sons along with several grandchildren. In August 2019, she earned a Ph.D. Biblical / Christian counseling, Friends International Christian University. Dr. Johnson is the Pastor of Saint Mary Freewill Baptist Church, Plant City, FL.

The Miraculous Exchange

"To appoint unto them that mourn in Zion, to give unto them beauty for ashes, the oil of joy for mourning, the garment of praise for the spirit of heaviness; that they might be called trees of righteousness, the planting of the LORD, that he might be glorified." (Isaiah 61:3)

The Lord creates an individual plan to develop areas in our lives that are broken and filled with loss, distrust, and disappointment, especially, in the secret places not easily seen nor the beauty revealed while in our fiery trials. Often, we understand there are different ashes, even with positive outcomes. Upon changing our vernacular, ashes represent dead and toxic places in our walk with God. He desires us to be transformed into a new creation rather than wallow. We appreciate the ashes when we remove the residue of the burned or dead relationships and careers. Revitalization happens by exchanging negative substances of bitterness, unforgiveness, and resentment for receipt of healing, peace, and a joyful future.

Life comes with many challenges beyond our control, predisposition of loss, and discouragements that affect us physically, spiritually, or emotionally. Our Hope is Christ is the only Life Changer. He turns our pain into Beauty. He heals our ugly scars, transforming our lives for His Glory.

Miraculously, our ashes nourish others to demonstrate our connectivity. Jesus turns chaos into calmness, bitterness into betterment, painful holes in our hearts into wholeness through His Word, Our Faith, and His Righteousness! The miracle occurs during the exchange process. Therefore, an important decision needs to be made. Do we continue to hold onto our past hurts, mistakes, and disappointments, or do we move forward to receive His "Blessed Assurance" of complete devotion of healing, love, and full of promises for tomorrow? Jesus will exceed our expectations, if we hold on to our faith for the arrival of the miraculous Joy in the Morning!

Rowena Jones

is an SVP in Technology for the one of largest banks in the US, an entrepreneur and founder of multiple businesses, a real estate investor, and more. Connect with her on Clubhouse and Instagram @RoeJonology

Favor the Widows

After losing my beloved husband to brain cancer, I was lost. I missed our life together. Life is full of adventure, love, laughter, and fulfillment. When your life was lived by two people as one, it's hard to even wake up in the morning after such a devastating loss. I immersed myself into work 24x7 to prevent grief from reaching in. It seemed I stopped living.

Then, a pivoting circumstance in my life forced me to find a new purpose in life for one.

My late husband always lived life setting mini goals. Small successes shorten a daunting endeavor and motivate you to keep pushing for the next. I applied the same approach with my new intended purpose. I searched for endeavors I could be passionate about once more. I honor my husband by continuing to do things he can be proud of in me.

I took solace in knowing that God favored widows. I focused on the manifestation of His graces in my life one at a time until I've come to count on them daily. Knowing I can rely on His protection gave me confidence. I found courage in knowing He will guide and look after me. I started with a small goal of learning something new that led to starting a business leveraging my newly acquired knowledge. I continued the same pattern until now I appreciate waking up to every new day full of hope and excitement of new experiences and blessings.

I continue to grieve my husband daily. He is in my thoughts several times a day in everything I do. Thoughts of him no longer bring debilitating pain but gratefulness of a life lived with him. My days are now filled with hope, courage, and endeavors that honor my husband.

Candy J

@ www.peacebestill.online

Author, Writer, Self-Love Coach, and Motivational Speaker. I have had many trials in life I overcame by knowing and understanding the true love of God. I have been gifted the gift of compassion to see others walk in success and know God's love and freedom.

Peace Be Still

"And he awoke and rebuked the wind and said to the sea, "Peace! Be Still" And the wind ceased and there was a great calm." (Mark 4:39 ESV)

I've had many trials in my life and the one thing I know is that we can have the peace and joy that God offers even in our mourning. We mourn many things in life such as losing jobs, friends, family, relationships, and much more. But the question I once asked God was how do I find His peace and joy amid mourning? How do I find it when my own heart was hurting?

Where is this peace that surpasses all understanding and this joy that gives us strength? God has shown me they are both heavily interlocked, always available, and waiting for us to just take it. But it's still all up to us.

God's peace is that inner calm given to us by God that rests within our hearts and removes all fear, worry, and anxious feelings that will also bring about joy within our hearts. Joy will then give us the strength to carry on despite any conflicts.

God gives it, but it's up to us to take it by stepping into his presence, communicating with him, and understanding he is sovereign and that everything is in the palm of his hands. He created it, he owns it, and he controls it. He loves you, wants what's best for you, and will not fail you. Always trust his process because even if you can't see him or feel him, he's there. His sovereignty is powerful and always there.

Reach for his love and you'll always find his presence, find his presence and you will always find his peace, find his peace and you'll always find his joy, find his joy and you'll always have his strength to rise above and make it through whatever life gives you.

Theresa Jordan

is a motivational speaker for Women's Conferences/Workshops and the Founder of Sisters Encouraging Sisters. She is a coach for Ultimate Coaching E change, she was born to motivate, and empower women through encouragement, which causes them to walk into their purpose and calling in life deliberately and unapologetically. Her favorite quote is by the late Dr. Maya Angelou," I've learned that people will forget what you said, people will forget what you did, but people will never forget how you made them feel.

Website: Triumphantmagazine.com Facebook: Triumphant Magazine Instagram: Triumphantmagazine_national YouTube: Triumphant Magazine Show Host Theresa Jordan

God Has Done Great Work in Me, and He Is the Author and Finisher of My Faith

"Being confident of this very thing, that he which hath begun a good work in you will perform it until the day of Jesus Christ:" (Philippians 1:6)

I have experienced many challenges in my life, but I am grateful I don't look like what I have been through. When I evaluate my own life, I can honestly say, "God has been good because He turns my midnight into day." The Lord has proven repeatedly His faithfulness toward me; therefore, I will continue to trust and depend on His Word. I know we serve a God that cannot lie, and He is a promise keeper. The Lord has spoken promises over me, and each promise will be manifested into my life. I know He will rock my world and blow my mind. According to 1 Corinthians 2:9, God's Word tells me, *"But as it is written, eyes hath not seen, nor ears heard, neither have entered into the heart of man, the things which God hath prepared for them that love him."*

I know the things the Lord has in store for me will affect this world. I do not doubt that the Lord knows that I will remember to give Him the honor, glory, and praise for the rest of my life. I will stay focused despite my circumstances. God has assured me, Theresa, "If you have faith as a grain of mustard seed, I can move mountains." My Faith can get me through the darkest of times. Experiences have shown me I can go through the fire and come out not smelling like smoke. My Faith can take me to places I never imagined would be possible for me. For I know the God that has begun a great work in me. My God is the author and the finisher so He will finish what He has begun in my life.

Cheryl Kehl

*is a minister, Chaplain, published author, and more.
Connect with her on Facebook, Cheryl Kehl.*

Created to Win

"To appoint unto them that mourn in Zion, to give unto them beauty for ashes, the oil of joy for mourning, the garment of praise for the spirit of heaviness; that they might be called trees of righteousness, the planting of the LORD, that he might be glorified." (Isaiah 61:3)

The last 2 years have been rough for us all with much pain and suffering. As we look back and see what God has kept us from and brought us through, we give Him praise. I have learned as I have matured to understand that life will not always be a bed of roses. We all have days we feel like giving up. As we are going through tough times, we sometimes think it will take us out. But God…When you find yourself in hard issues it does make you feel a little weary. But think back on all the things that God has brought you through in the past. He is still the same God and cares so much for you.

We do not always understand why things turn so sour sometimes. Life seems to throw a lot of punches at us. When trouble comes close together it does land a little different on us physically and emotionally. But God promises to give us beauty for our ashes. If we continue to trust and believe, he will give us a time for rejoicing. Nothing gives me more joy than knowing I serve a God that can and will turn any situation around.

Remember you won!

Marnie Lacy

It's my pleasure to work with Dr. Vernessa Blackwell again. I enjoyed playing with my 2 grandsons and by the way I have 5 adult kids I love dearly. I'm trying to live my best life. Thank you again.

Daddy's Girl

I heard your voice in the wind today and I turn to see your face.

The warmth of the wind caressed me as I stood silently in place.

I felt your touch in the sun today as its warmth filled the sky.

I closed my eyes for your embrace and my spirit soared high.

I saw your eyes in the windowpane as I watched the falling rain.

It seemed as each raindrop fell it quietly said your name daddy.

I held you close in my heart today it made me feel complete.

You may have died but you are not gone.

You will always be a part of me as long as the sun shines, the wind blows, the rain falls.

You will live on inside of me forever for that is all my heart knows

I love you daddy. Keep watching over me.

Karen Lewis

is an instructional coach, published author, content creator, adoring wife, and loving mother of two adults and 1 gorgeous granddaughter. In her spare time, she enjoys plant-based cooking, spending time with her family, and traveling. Share her journey of recuperation on YouTube: Recuperate With Me

WHEN GOD INTERRUPTS YOUR LIFE

"The Lord will work out His plans for my life - for your faithful love, O Lord, endures forever. Don't abandon me, for you made me." (Psalms 138:8 NLT)

Recently, I had a serious health crisis! The big C! Although when I went to the emergency room, had a colonoscopy, and ultimately emergency surgery all four-days days, I had no idea that I even had Cancer. I could have used this moment to dwell on what happened at home recuperating for the past month.

Instead, I focused on the dreams I once pursued and had almost given up on. When God hears the desires of your heart, He is determined to see you through. Psalms 138:8 from the NLT version says *"The Lord will work out His plans for my life - for your faithful love, O Lord, endures forever. Don't abandon me, for you made me"*.

I trust that God saw I was on a path where my dreams would be deferred. He is not a man He should lie. This interruption is merely part of His plan for my life as I do not have cancer, nor do I need chemo. If ever you are to go through a crisis, remember that as a Believer, God has you in His loving arms and will see you through it all! As of this writing, I am still recuperating, but God's got me!

Dr. Tina D. Lewis

is a serial entrepreneur with over 30 years of successful experience in business, sales, marketing, and revenue generation. Dr. Tina is the Founder of the 6 Figure Incubator, a membership-based community that nurtures entrepreneurs and their businesses into a solid 6 figure cash cow. Visit The6FigureIncubator.com

It's Not Funny!
"Count it all JOY." (James 1:2)

Have you ever laughed at something that wasn't funny? or laughed and someone shouted "It's not funny? I have. It was funny at the time but in retrospect, what I found humorous, someone else experienced mourning. It's crazy right. You see, I love to laugh. I get it from my mommy. LITERALLY! She is always cracking jokes, laughing at her jokes, and making fun of herself and others. She's an incredible young lady. Love her to pieces. I learned a lot from my mom. I believed she was a magician. She took a little and made a WHOLE lot! She taught me how to find Joy in the Morning. I lost the person who was my oxygen. It was my maternal grandfather. He was a shrewd businessman, a jokester as well. My mom helped me through it. She taught me Joy in the Mourning.

My mom was in a near-fatal car accident. She was hospitalized for three whole months. Her life has not been the same since. I honestly lost a piece of her because of that life experience. Even though she's different, I've witnessed through her misfortune Joy in the Mourning.

I've been through a lot of challenges in my life. Some things I am not proud of and some I was still embarrassed to share. Despite it all, my mom has been my rock and has illustrated and led by example how to find Joy in the Mourning.

NO MATTER WHAT happens, life is a cycle. Either you are going into mourning, in the middle of mourning, coming out of mourning, or know someone in mourning. #FACTS! Therefore, you have a warning, a little foresight. You know you're going there and what you do at this destination or truck stop if you will, is up to you!

I highly suggest, no I beseech you. To Find J O Y amid the Mourning because afterward remembering your mourning will bring an indescribable JOY!

Dr. Maribel Lopez

is an author, inspirational speaker, and ordained minister born on the beautiful island of Puerto Rico. Lover of Jesus and life! Her purpose is to empower and help individuals heal from the lies plagued and imprinted by childhood sexual abuse and rape. You can find her at www.drmaribellopez.com

HOPE

"I lift my eyes to the mountains— where does my help come from? My help comes from the LORD, the Maker of heaven and earth."
(Psalm 121: 1-2 NIV)

Picture this, Chicago, 1988, Aha! Just kidding, we just recently said goodbye to Betty White, from The Golden Girls, a program that brought much joy to my life. Discriminatory at times, it also brought joy and laughter. This will make sense later I promise, I just couldn't help it.

When I came from the beautiful Island of Puerto Rico, I didn't have many friends. I was bullied in school. This young man who took a liking to me developed a true friendship with me and we hung out. He became my protector; if anyone tried to bother me, he would defend me. Shortly thereafter, he was killed by gang violence. I was devasted.

Right before I met my husband, I lost another friend. I was angry with God, and I asked Him. Why? You forgot about me, Lord. By now I thought, I was supposed to be happily married living the "American dream". That is not what happened. Instead, I fell into depression and a sense of hopelessness. Doubting whether I was important enough to God, feeling like he forgot about me.

During my time of grief, I asked, prayed, and waited. I laughed (hence, me watching the golden girls) and kept joy in my life. "Rejoice always," says the Lord (1 Thessalonians 5:16). I still miss the people I loved. Jesus wiped my tears away and brought joy and strength to my life. Through the study of the Word of God, I received hope, healing, and joy.

You too can have the hope of hopes and live a fully abundant life in Jesus.

Dr. Fikisha Marée

is a life coach, published author, pastoral counselor, and certified mediator. Connect with her at: https://linktr.ee/fikishamaree

HAPPY DESERT BLUES

"Trust in the Lord with all your heart and lean not to your understanding."
(Proverbs 3:5)

Often, after you find your niche, develop good relationships, and groove to a rhythm of fulfillment and life, suddenly trauma strikes. No more happy tunes, now swallowed up in a desert abyss, consumed of blues. You wonder how I got here, battling fight or flight, trying to figure a way out. Well, just like you, life has happened several times. I found myself covered in grains of sand (life circumstances). Every grain causes deep scars of hopelessness and confusion. I was short on oxygen, due to the inhalation of desert particles of heartbreak and doubt.

Slowly, I climbed out of the desert abyss. Instead of trying to figure it out and regain control, I let go! I shut the door on Why Me, and embraced Why Not Me? I let God use me during my time of pain and grief. I became stronger than ever, armed with His Word, blossoming like Spring leaves. Grief may cause confusion, but trust in the Lord. Permit God to dwell in your heart and replace the pain, with His peace. You'll never know why trauma summoned you to the desert abyss. I hope one day you reminisce and be happy you experienced the blues, because many are called, but God only chooses a few.

Brandee Martin

affectionately known as Ms. "BJ" Martin is a Best-Selling Author, Singer/ Songwriter, C.E.O. and E ecutive Producer of "Snails with No Shells". Ms. BJ Martin is an advocate for Mental Health Awareness and has been highlighted for her valued presence and philanthropic leadership.

Email: <u>info@iammsbjmartin.com</u> Books: msbjmartin.com

Healing "Daddy Issues"

Yep, I still had "Daddy Issues" at the age of 39. Forty was coming fast and I knew that I was ready for change. I was in my kitchen washing dishes. I was on the phone with my friend. In that moment I was thinking, there has to be more to life than this. I asked God for an upgrade in my life. I had no idea what that upgrade entailed. I quickly discovered that a major part of that upgrade I wanted and needed was ME.

Sometimes, we want things outside of us to be upgraded. Our houses, cars, jobs, children, etc. but we need to make the changes inside of us first. I digress. It was time to finally resolve the issues I had with my dad. I grew up without my father in my life. He paid child support, but he was not present. I did not realize how much that affected me until I was an adult. I thought I was good. My actions showed otherwise. Shortly thereafter I felt like I was going back into a depression phase.

But that was not it. God was bringing out and stirring up emotions of abandonment, loneliness, and sadness just to name a few so, that I could heal. My dad contacted me often in the past, but I was not ready. I called my dad and I cried. We talked about all the emotions and thoughts I had. We healed together. It took time but we did it. Because I did the work my relationships with the men in my life improved including my relationship with my sons. I chose to heal. I chose ME.

Dr. Celeste Johnson-Matheson

is an Executive Liaison Officer with the US Army, Training and Doctrine Command, Best Selling Inspirational Author, and Businesswoman. Celeste plans to establish a global non-profit organization to provide books to children in underserved communities. Celeste has a Master's degree in Business Psychology.
https://keepmenearthecross.com/ and https://kidsinneeddreamsuccess.com/

FINDING JOY IN YOUR BROKENESS

"These things have I spoken to you, that My joy may remain in you, and that your joy may be full." (John 15:11 NJKV)

Life comes with its shares of challenges, disappointments, and heartaches. Life has a way of knocking us off our feet when we least expect it. I will refer to this period in our lives as "Our Brokenness." The period of brokenness can occur when grieving, in pain, feels hopeless, fearful, depressed, unloved, and undervalued.

All of us will experience brokenness during our lifetime. It's the period when our strength is tested, our faith wavers, and our hearts are troubled. I remember as a young child discovering that both my grandparents were found deceased. Later in life, I was devastated by having a miscarriage and the tragic death of my youngest brother. How do you find Joy in such tragedies when you're emotionally, physically, and spiritually depleted? One way you can reverse brokenness is by replacing it with Joy. Joy means "a feeling of great pleasure and happiness." Joy can be found by reassuring yourself in your brokenness; there is a great opportunity for you to find Joy again!

Joy in knowing you are rescued from the challenges and pain from yesterday and given a new day for greater love, greater peace, and greater happiness. During your "brokenness," be mindful it's only temporary, and that Joy will always prevail even when you don't feel it or see it. Connect with your emotions by doing positive things such as praying, practicing positive affirmations, and doing acts of kindness for others. Find something daily that makes you smile, feel excited, loved, and happy. The brokenness in your life was meant for you to endure temporarily, but JOY is intended to be everlasting. Seek God, trust God, and believe you will laugh, smile, and rejoice again.

Dr. Y'Londa Mitchell

is the owner of a counseling and wellness private practice. She is a Licensed Professional Counselor, Board Certified Counselor, and Registered Yoga Teacher. She served in the US Army and the Iraq war.
And she is a proud alumnus of Kentucky State University and Tennessee State University.

Grief to Gratitude

"Blessed are those that mourn, for they shall be comforted."
(Matthew 5:4)

How do we move forward when everything around us is crashing down? That is exactly where I found myself on September 14, 2021. Death. Grief. There is no way around it. But why do we struggle with acceptance? My grief was unique because it was disenfranchised. Suicide grief. It's the grief that leaves no answers, only questions. To complicate matters we had a virtual memorial service with technical difficulties. I was in pain with an invisible barrier during my final goodbye to my friend. I was left feeling cheated, angry, and alone.

I'm not sure when I turned the corner towards gratitude, but it happened. I finally smiled and noticed little moments of gratitude. One day I saw a white butterfly and felt a sense of peace, another day a rainbow. People say it all the time, but grief is LOVE. I thought about our shared moments. I thought about our phone calls and shared secrets. I had the honor of having a friend, a brother, and someone that loved me.

I know that it is hard. Take time to reflect on those good moments. Continue to remember their legacy. You don't need closure from grief because love is forever. Death doesn't stop LOVE. Just know that you can still love and miss someone while moving forward with your life.

Take comfort today knowing that the sun will shine again even while tears are falling. One day, maybe tomorrow or next month, but in due time God will bring the pain to an end. You don't have to endure it alone. God's grace and strength will be the source of your victory. I wish you healing on your journey. Be kind to yourself. You are experiencing one of the greatest gifts of life which is LOVE.

Bethzali Mongare

is starting "Pressure Washing Queen;" a residential and commercial pressure washing company in Waco Te as. Bethzali wrote a Christian fiction book entitled Don Miguel. You can find her and connect with her on linkedin. ee/betsymongare

I Am Restored Piece By Piece Daily

"Therefore say: 'This is what the Sovereign Lord says: I will gather you from the nations and bring you back from the countries where you have been scattered, and I will give you back the land of Israel again..." (Ezekiel 11:17-2017 NIV)

Twenty-twenty-one was the worst year of my life; I went through so many things at once, so much pain and grief. I had known God throughout my life, but I felt like I had become too comfortable and departed from Him. I felt I was scattered everywhere into puzzle pieces.

Like a puzzle, God puts a piece of me together every day and works on my restoration and healing so I won't not be scattered but whole in Him. But in my pain, I knocked at Jesus' door and He brought me back again. I realized that God never abandoned me; He loved me so much He waited patiently for me to come back.

I now enjoy and look forward to hearing from God daily in bible verses, worship, songs, and messages from the Pastor, TBN network, or an encouraging YouTube message. God is molding me into the person He created me to be. I am happy God is guiding my path and I look forward to an Amazing blessed 2022.

We cannot change our heart of stone by ourselves; it must happen by God supernaturally when He gives us a heart transplant. God's desire for every human is that we become like His Son.

We can become like Jesus only when we allow God to rid us of our old, hardened sinful hearts and give us new Christ softened hearts. Jesus called it being born again. Psalm 30:11 Lord "You turned my mourning into joyful dancing. *You have taken away my clothes of mourning and clothed me with Joy.*"

Bianca Moore

is a Cyber Security Engineer, published author, and Certified Zumba Instructor. She enjoys mentoring children and helping new Cyber Security professionals advance in their careers. Connect with her on Facebook, Author Bianca Moore, and at iamauthorbiancamoore@gmail.com

Stop Interfering in God's Business

"Be still and know that I am God. I will be exalted among the nations; I will be exalted in the earth" (Psalms 46:10 NIV)

What is God trying to tell us here? Briefly, He is saying He's got it. Stop interfering with God's plans for your life and let Him handle it. The more we interfere with this, the more we hinder our blessings. God can't work like this with our constant interference. He doesn't need our help.

When worry and frustration set in, we go into a state of "how can I fix this?" What we don't realize is God already has it worked out. How many times have we gotten into trouble and have no idea how we got out of it unscathed? That was God's protection over our lives. I get it. It's easy to tell someone not to worry and harder for them to not do it. Worry is a natural emotion, and we all are guilty of doing it.

Have you ever had a difficult manager and wanted to quit your job? I'm willing to bet that many people have left their current positions because of difficult people. What you don't realize is God sees you struggling with this, and He will deal with that situation for you. Every obstacle you endure is being worked out for your good. I have witnessed first-hand the way God has moved people out of my way.

Have you prayed for something that hasn't been answered yet? Like the scripture says, Be Still, and know that I am God. He hasn't forgotten you. Be patient. Just trust him and don't worry. Like I said earlier, He's got it!!

Dr. Barbara J. Neely

is the owner and CEO of Mama's Brown Sugar an all- natural skincare line. Neely is a former military spouse of nineteen and a mother of a son. She is active in her community and believes in giving back and serving others. She loves reading and teaching others how to care for their skin and understand what they are putting on their bodies. She is very passionate about encouraging and supporting other women. You can find her products here @www.mamasbrownsugar.com

The Two Faces of Grief

"He heals the brokenhearted and binds up their wounds."
(Psalms 147:3 ESV)

Death and divorce evoke very similar feelings of loss. Both involve the pain of loss, and often the loss of your self-identity. I have walked through losing parents and losing a spouse through a divorce and can tell you I experienced all the stages of grief and still, through each loss, God has walked alongside me, and when I felt weak, he carried me.

Sometimes though both types of death, we can feel abandoned, depressed, and lose our identity, but our identity doesn't reside in man, but Christ. When reality sinks because your loved one isn't coming back, the pain and fear can be crippling, but I am reminded that people will leave you and let you down, but God is in the same place he always has been in and will never leave you.

Walking through the grief of loss felt like the pain would never end, but I have experienced the comfort and healing of Christ during these traumatic times.

Revelation 21:4 ESV: *"He will wipe away every tear from their eyes, and death shall be no more, neither shall there be mourning, nor crying, nor pain anymore, for the former things have passed away."*

Have faith in knowing that God hears every cry and cares about our pain and hurt. He will heal the hurt in your heart and give you peace to face another day. In this season of grief, I take comfort in knowing I'm never alone and there is nothing too hard for the Lord. Our hope comes from an unchanged, faithful God. God does not set a timeline for grief, and everything that happens in our lives passes through God's hands.

Dr. Thomasina "Denice" Nicholas

is a wife, mother, grandmother, retired Army Veteran, and social worker. She's the Best-Selling Author of a Feast in the Desert (Keys to Spiritual Readiness), Co- Author of Finding Joy in the Journey, and founder of "At the Table Global Ministries. "Thomasina holds a B.S.in Organizational Management/Christian Counseling from Covenant University and Liberty University, M.A., and a D.MIN. from Ministry International Institute.

THE PRESS THAT LEADS TO THE OIL OF GLADNESS"

"To appoint unto them that mourn in Zion, to give unto them beauty for ashes, the oil of joy for mourning, the garment of praise for the spirit of heaviness; that they might be called trees of righteousness, the planting of the LORD, that he might be glorified." (Psalms 61:3)

In one's course of life, conditions arise that we had not signed up for. Daily we go about our lives in a state of mind that leaves us in what I would like to call "The Press." The PRESS comes into play when we allow areas of our life to hold us captive, and we succumb to them. The enemy wants us to give ourselves to these changes and take our eyes off God, the author and finisher of our faith, to focus on what is in front of us rather than our faith walk.

However, the Master Teacher has a more gracious plan for our outcome than demise. Satan's lies would bring us to these presses: depression, oppression, regress, and distress. These are all stages of weakening our faith vital to the Process and the plan of God for our lives.

You see God allows us to go through the process of the press and the pressure so we can master the circumstance we are facing. And like the olive tree which is cold-pressed and moved into position for the essence of the best oil extracted, God wants the best out of us. So, you see the pressures of life are necessary for us to make it through the "press of life."

Here is the formula: PRESSURE – IT= No Testimony nor Oil of Gladness. If humankind never pressed, we could never give our IT (internal testimony) nor will we be gifted with our special anointing from God, and like an olive tree that has never matured, it will eventually die. On the other hand, PRESS(URE) + INTERNAL TESTIMONY=Progress to move forward toward the beauty and destiny for which God designed.

Shywanna Nock

is a mother, published author, and inspirational speaker. Shywanna has her associate degree in Business Administration/Finance. Connect with her on Facebook Shywanna Nock Author Page, and at shywannanock.com

Don't Stop, Don't Quit

"For we walk by faith, not by sight." (2 Corinthians 5:7)

We all have experienced a downfall in our lives. We often feel that the obstacles that come our way are very challenging. The overwhelming part of the challenge is we don't know the results of our situation. The scripture, "we walk by faith and not by sight," sets the tone for us to trust God and not focus on what we see.

Different obstacles cause us to stumble and fall to our knees.

We have to get up, dust off ourselves, and get back in the fight. We lose track of the path that God set before us because we're focused on what is in front of us. We have to pray and seek God, even when we think he is not there.

God will never leave us in times of trouble. We have to keep pushing and pressing our way.

We have to show up even when we don't feel like it. Remember that no matter the situation, we can make it. God has equipped us with everything that we need.

God is behind us saying, keep going. You got this. You are in it to win it. I didn't bring you this far, for you to give up. You can make it, and I am with you every step of the way. No matter what you face. Don't stop and don't quit.

Dr. Adrienne Reed Oliver

is a native of Alton, IL, a mother of two lovely children, and an author of two books. She has her Master's Degree in Ed Leadership and currently works as a Curriculum Specialist in IL. She is a singer, songwriter, artist, and motivational speaker.
https://www.amazon.com/Shut-God-Talkin-Adrienne- Reed-Oliver/dp/1520889267

The Art of Letting Go

"The Lord is close to the brokenhearted and saves those who are crushed in the spirit." (Psalm 34:18 NIV)

"I can't do this by myself!" These six words were my new reality...until I let go. I was crushed when my husband died suddenly of an aneurysm. I was a single mom "again"!

My first husband was brutally abusive. My baby and I were blessed to escape alive. But this marriage was not supposed to end. It was supposed to last a lifetime.

My Ceddy, my love, died in my arms. When he died, I died. I didn't want to live. This was too hard. I'd finally found true love for it to be snatched away.

Boy was I angry! The breaking point was when I realized that life was still going on and that I wasn't going to heaven soon.

Eventually, I got up from the slump I was in. I stood before the Lord naked and beat up, with my guard down. The healing and letting go didn't start until I forgave. I blamed God, so I had to forgive Him.

I had to realize that He took my love because he was ready. I had to forgive Ceddy for leaving me, and I had to forgive myself for thoughts or things I should or shouldn't have done. The real healing didn't take place until I let go of all hurts, regrets, blame, and shame.

The story of a toddler and a stick helped me to heal, understand and forgive. A toddler had a stick. His older brother took the stick from him. The toddler had a fit and screamed. The brother ignored his screams and broke the stick. To the toddlers' delight, the stick glowed. As you heal remember, God takes things away from us to give us better, but we have to trust him by letting go.

Issata Oluwadare

is a dynamic leader with over ten years of higher education leadership experience. She is also a content creator, bestselling author, entrepreneur, motivational speaker, certified life coach and consultant for women in leadership and business, and founder of The EZ Breezy Life. Learn more at www.ezbreezy.life and www.issatao.com.

The God Who Sees Me

"The eyes of the Lord are on the righteous, and his ears are attentive to their cry." (Psalms 34:15 NIV)

She stepped into the room like an angel. Full of bubbly energy. She was from Cuba where she used to be a doctor and was now a respiratory therapist within the same system that my child was hospitalized.

As I sat there holding Emmanuel with over 30 wires flowing from his body, I felt heavy. My spirit felt heavy. My eyes felt heavy. The burden on my shoulders felt heavy. We had already lost his sister, and it took everything in me to keep the faith that God could save my baby.

The woman paused and said she knew she was violating protocol, but felt compelled to share her faith in me, and the importance of taking care of myself, even if I was going through a hard time. She talked about these nutrients she took and how they helped her feel 20 years younger. I felt refreshed just being around her. Whatever she had, I knew I wanted it. I bought the vitamins and kept in touch with her for the remainder of Emmanuel's hospitalization. That singular encounter gave me the boost in my faith, strength, and resources I desperately needed for the rest of the journey.

If you are passing through difficulty this season, I want to encourage you to fix your eyes on Psalm 34. Pray to the God who sees and hears you when no one else can. In our darkest moments, he sends help from the most unexpected places. Amen.

Sheena Vendoria Parson

My entire world changed the day the Fugitive Task Force surrounded our home. As I write, I can still taste the salt from my children's tears. After two years in that cell, I discovered that my purpose is to pave the way to freedom for others.www.amendrestart.com

AMEN'D

"For I know the thoughts that I think toward you, saith the Lord, thoughts of peace, and not of evil, to give you an expected end". (Jeremiah 29:11)

It's cold here. I mean, I'm thankful for what I have. Some don't even have the luxury of this metal bunk bed or new friends every few days. For that alone, I'm blessed. I just pray the heat kicks on soon; I can see my breath.

It's cold here. Sounds of heavy keys jingle through the halls while arguing can be heard through the vent. It's true, you don't need a phone for the most important call. As soon as I mouthed, "Abba, I need YOU." The message was sent.

Abba, it's cold here. Nobody knows me. They have read and assume I am what THEY'VE written never mind my intermission. As I cried out, He told me to allow them to ASSUME their position then He softly continued giving me this mission.

Upon release, I was Divinely Ordered to change laws and reconcile families. I was ordered to Feed and Clothe His people. I was told to Lay Hands on the sick and they would recover, IN JESUS' NAME- no other.

The I AM God became everything. Though I wrote the vision and made it plain, the plan was bigger than me. He gave me this mission and I wrote the vision to lead us BOTH to victory.

Leona D. G. Partis

is a Retired Air Force, a Dept of Defense Civilian, and REALTOR® in Southern, MD. Leona's business is built on integrity, knowledge, and trust. Leona brings a wealth of knowledge and experience in coaching, mentoring, and executive talent management.

Post-Traumatic Stress Disorder

"For his anger endureth but a moment, in his favor is life: Weeping May endure for a night but joy cometh in the morning". (Psalms 30:5)

It was a cool, sunny morning in Washington, DC. I was Active-Duty United States Air Force with six years of service. I was completing routine morning duties when the phone rang, and the spouse of my coworker was on the phone telling everyone to turn on the TV. A few of us huddled around a small TV and to our surprise we saw a plane hitting the World Trade Center in New York.

As we continued to watch, we saw another plane hit the second World Trade Center tower; we were all in shock. I later heard someone running through the halls saying the base was locked down, and we needed to get accountability of our personnel. There was news of another imminent attack, and it would be in DC.

We all gathered near our 4th-floor window and looked across the Potomac River. We saw smoke coming from across the river and then heard on the TV that the Pentagon was hit by a plane. Everyone was in disbelief; we all knew people who worked at the Pentagon and all we could do was look at the smoke and TV for more news. Later we heard there was another plane crash in Pennsylvania. Life had changed for America, and we all knew the military we served in had changed.

The attacks in NY, DC, and Pennsylvania meant war was imminent. As personnel, I was told to report to the office later that night for casualty assistance team support for the Pentagon. I thought this day and night would never end. As a military member, we regularly experience Post Traumatic Stress Disorder (PTSD). However, on that day all of America experienced the trauma of PTSD and struggles with it daily using prayer, meditation, and family support.

T.K. Peoples

an educator, librarian, and best-selling author of children and adult books. She is a proud alumni of The University of Georgia and grew up in Crawford GA. Now, Jonesboro, GA has been her home for over 20 years.

T.K. always keeps God first and everything else fall in place. Follow her on all social media platforms @anortbooks.
Website: www.anortbooks.com

Repossessions to God's Double Blessings!

"Wealth and riches are in their houses, and their righteousness endures forever." (Psalm 112:3)

Flashback...two young babies, 6 months and 18 months, and my husband had lost his job for several months now. We woke up to get the boys ready for daycare one cool morning. At our door, we see that our car is gone and everything in it! Papers, our children's car seats, Diapers, etc... All gone! I felt as if the wind had knocked out my chest.

With my husband not working, the only income came from my substitute teaching job at the local school. That would be $1800 per month. Daycare took half of that. The decision was made to pay the most essential rent and electricity. The government's food stamps provided food.

The bills piled up. The water company would turn the water off, and we would get the tools to turn it back on as soon as they left. The car payment was months behind. We had heard the horror stories of cars being repossessed during the night. So, we strategically parked the vehicles making it difficult for any tow company. One day, we forgot! Quietly in the night, the repo truck whisked the car away.

How could two college graduates end up like this? I was devastated and cried for weeks. I was embarrassed when people asked about the Ford SUV Truck. My husband and I grew up in the church and knew how to have faith and continue following God's words. At the lowest point in our lives, we held on to faith and prayed for better days. Over the years, we have been blessed to prosper and grow. God has given us more than enough. We have cars paid for and were recently given CARS because the family no longer needed it. Joy will come in the morning! Trust God!

Troy Rawlings

www.TroyRawlingsLive.com
Host, Comedian, Actor, Speaker, and Author Troy Rawlings' mission is simple, "to help men & women communicate better in love." Troy's comedy and hosting style bring his amazing writing, improvisational, and production skills to the masses every time he performs on a stage, on TV, or on Radio!

"Night Cries & Sunlight"

I've heard it said before those words can become flesh. So, if that's the case, then it makes perfect sense that we can live out words. It then would be possible for us to walk out the reality of our phrases. Case in point, I recall nights where I'd stare at the white ceiling of my bedroom. Pushing my yearning past the paint, plaster, drywall, wooden beams, and tar, bursting into the deep night sky. Piercing through stars and galaxies into a mystic, majestic heaven to sit at the feet of my heavenly father, just to ask...why?

Why am I alone, and so lonely? Why is the electricity off again, and why is the phone off? Should I get another job? Is it time to finally hit the streets and hustle? I'm 14, where are my parents? I should quit. I'm so tired. I'm sick and tired. As the moonlight illuminated my bedroom, and I lay flat on my back, I could feel the teardrops leave the corners of my eyes, run down the sides of my head, and fill my ears.

I would complain and talk, reason, and cry until I fell asleep. Then, like clockwork, the Sun would wake me up for a new day. All shadows of fear and doubt would be gone. I would walk around my house and open every window.

The Sun would not be quiet! And neither should I. It was time for school. It was time to learn, have fun, and laugh. The excitement of the new day would always overpower the tears of the night before. And somehow, it got better. The Sun never quit on me, so neither did I.

Debra Riddlespriger

is an Evangelist and Psalmist, Debra is a proud mother and grandmother, an actress, aspiring author, and poet. Having experienced various types of losses of her own, she is committed to the mission of helping others overcome and achieve through her ministry,
"Life to the Full."

RESTORE AND RESET

And after you have suffered a little while, the God of all grace, who has called you to his eternal glory in Christ, will himself restore, confirm, strengthen, and establish you."
(1 Peter 5:10 ESV)

Father God, you have always been with me, and I am grateful! You preceded me in every tragedy and escorted me out to every victory. You have always proven yourself to me through Your power, Your understanding, Your grace, Your mercy, and Your provision. Great is Your faithfulness! Now, it is my turn to prove my complete trust in You, no matter how difficult it may seem.

Yes, I see You in it all! You have shown me amid the most tragic times, that ALL things work together for the good of those that love You! You have shown me so many people attached to my commitment to You and my faith in You. Please, Lord, touch the lives of those who are attached to my journey.

I am casting all of my cares and I fully surrender my will to Yours. When I look back, your way has always been the solution to every challenge.

You are The Great Restorer! I am all the way in and I trust in You. I know you will help me through this. I know you will give me peace throughout every storm, I know you are positioning me to receive every promise. I give You full reign! I give You the glory for it all!

In Jesus' Name Amen

LaTonya Kirksey-Roberts

was born on January 19, 1979 in a small town in The Southeast coast of Brunswick Georgia.
LaTonya is a mighty Woman of Faith. She Is a woman of God who loves working in the Kingdom.
LaTonya is now a successful business owner whose passion and love is for bettering her community. She is a Georgia life insurance agent and a Certified Notary Public. She's a board-certified credit consultant, Business Coach, and Amazon #1 Best selling Author. She is a devoted wife, a mother, and an entrepreneur.
LaTonya is active in her community and loves her community.

KEEP PUSHING

"God's mercies are new every morning and His compassions fail us not." (Psalm 30: 4-5)

"Sing praises unto the Lord, O you saints and give thanks unto His holy name. For his anger is but for a moment and His favor is for a lifetime. Weeping may tarry for the night, but joy comes with the morning."

Sometimes, we need to be restored through trials and tribulations. Restored means just like new. Only this can be done through the power of healing. God's miraculous healing power. Joy in the morning captivates the true essence of healing. And after you've healed, true love will flourish.

God reminds us that weeping may endure for a night, but joy comes in the morning. Hold steadfast to your faith. The word of God says it is impossible to please Him without Faith. Go through your trials and receive the strength from on High. Be strong in the Lord and the Power of His might. God gives you strength for another day.

As I'm writing this book, I thought about losing my mother. This was a gut-wrenching pain I struggled with. Losing your mother is not something I wish on my worst enemy. Though it's rough, the Lord is a lamp unto my feet and leads and guides me into exceeding Joy. This day is the day I laid my mother to rest. But I hear a quiet, still voice whispering, "Keep pushing". As quiet as the voice was, the words became bold, louder, and clear that I can't give up. You, reading this: Don't throw in the towel. In the presence of the Lord is fullness of joy for eternity. Because your JOY COMES IN THE MORNING.

Malissa T. Roberts

is the founder and leader of the Women After God's Own Heart Bible study group and a prospective author.
Malissa earned her MBA at Clark Atlanta University, continued post-graduate studies in education, earned an Ed.S. at Piedmont University, and serves as an educational leader in Georgia. Malissa is a native of Riviera Beach, Florida, and resides in Stockbridge, Georgia where she is a devoted wife to her husband, Dr. Rick Roberts, and mother of three children.
MalissaTysonRoberts@gmail.com

When Joy and Mourning Walk Hand in Hand

"To provide for those who mourn in Zion – to bestow on them a crown of beauty instead of ashes, the oil of joy instead of mourning, and a garment of praise instead of a spirit of despair. They will be called oaks of righteousness, a planting of the Lord for the display of His splendor." (Isaiah 61:3 NIV)

In the hospital room stood my dad, siblings, a dear friend of our family, and me. There, we encircled the bed of my mother, a strong, committed, diligent woman of faith in her final moments of life here on earth as cancer consumed her body. While singing, only paused by moments of prayer, something extraordinary, no, the supernatural was happening.

The experience, while gut-wrenchingly painful, in the atmosphere was something remarkable. I call it our beautiful awful. As one tear brushed the cheek of my mother, our beautiful awful was happening. It was as if the choirs of heaven were joining us in song, ushering in precious, sweet joy during the most difficult experience of our lives. There, in that room, the power of His presence was providing for us during our time of mourning, just as He promised. In our passage, we see joy and mourning sitting side by side, but can they occupy the same space, in the depths of who we are as people, in our very soul? The very essence of the two screams contradictory, impossible, and even improbable. But can they walk together and coexist, like two dear friends?

Our Lord is there, and when His presence fills the atmosphere, you can experience this joy even while mourning. Knowing this, you can praise Him for the blessing of the life of your loved one even during the momentary despair of loss. Will you trust Him to do the same for you? He promised to provide for you as you mourn and to bestow on you beauty for the ashes and the oil of joy during these painful and difficult seasons of life.

Ronnette Rock

was born and raised in Maryland. She has the pleasure of being the mother of four amazing young men ages, 31, 29,25, and 18, Brandon, Sean, Keenan, and Bryce. She has two grandchildren, Ava and Jude. She is married to a wonderful husband, Bryan and she Praises her life as it was constructed slowly, fearfully, graciously, and crafted in God's time.

Then Comes Resilience

"Fear thou not; for I am with thee be not dismayed; for I am thy God: I will strengthen thee; yea, I will help thee; yea, I will uphold thee with the right hand of my righteousness." (Isaiah 41:10-29)

I was always told I was a fighter from day one. I never knew that I had to fight until I became an adult. Nothing could have ever prepared me for the journey that was coming, that was filled with dark clouds and pain. A blessing did await but in God's time, and the path he was laying for me. Then and only then would I even know what he had in store for me.

My world took a turn when I entered the military. I was sexually assaulted at 19, and was Married by 20. I thought I was on top of the world, then My life took a painful turn with infidelities; I felt so broken and defeated. I was left pregnant, homeless, and with four beautiful kids and no financial nest to even guide me out of this mess. A sense of failure and shame washed over me. I was my kid's only Protector, and I couldn't let them down so I had to push depression and pain to the side and cry at night while they slept so that I could be the strong mommy at the light. I prayed a lot.

One day God answered. I left the shelter, graduated college, got a job, purchased a house, all because I renewed my faith, confidence, and self-esteem, which I thought I had lost. My kids are my heartbeats, and I will never give up because they were my bright lights through my hard storms. Then I met my true Soulmate, and another storm hit; I was diagnosed with cancer. My husband anchored for me and became my Rock, and never wavered. Today I'm free and blessed. I used to think God failed me only to know God prepared me to be strong and resilient to fight harder in love and faith.

Dr. Radiance Laveena-Nicole Rose

22-year combat veteran of the U.S. Air Force is professionally known as a Transformational Leader, Professor, Advocate, Executive Coach, and Entrepreneur, who is skilled in leadership & character development at various levels of management.

Faith On Fire

"I can do all things through Christ who strengthens me."
(Philippians 4:13)

Throughout my life, I have faced incredible adversities. From losing a mother at a young age to getting married & divorced, having multiple miscarriages, single parenting, carrying emotional baggage, struggling with feelings of abandonment, rejection, & unworthiness, having an identity crisis, a heart condition, surviving a stroke, traumatic brain injury (in the military), and beating cancer twice. I also suffer from anxiety and depression. As an educator and coach, most people who know me would say that I am energetic & laser-focused on helping others in the areas of personal & professional growth.

On March 7, 2020, I was in a bad car accident that drastically impacted my quality of life. A little more than a week later, the earth quaked with a global pandemic, and isolation and loneliness settled in. My mental health took a nosedive into the sea of a psychological abyss. On July 10, 2020, challenges and strife almost got the best of me. I was in a mental wilderness with seemingly no way out. I wondered if my life was worth living. Was my fate reduced to heartache, misery, and death? I contemplated suicide. Yes, this highly functioning, extroverted Christian woman began to question my existence. How could I help transform the lives of others and be unable to navigate through my own life? I was emotionally bankrupted. Thank God that's not how the chapter ended. God smiled on me and restored my faith in him. Prayer, faith, therapy, support of family & friends, and a willingness to persevere is how I made it through it all. Jesus, the Captain of my soul, anchored me. I don't know how my life's story will end, but I am encouraged, and I believe that God's got a blessing with my name on it.

LaTia N. S. Russell

LCSW is a wife, mother and co-captain of a multi- generational household. Indie author, and co-owner of Ties That Bind Publishing, LLC.
Website: https://tiesthatbindpublishing.com/ Linktree:
https://linktr.ee/TTBP20
Facebook: https://www.facebook.com/Ties-That-Bind- Publishing-107099741322396/ Instagram:

The Day My Father Died...

"For the Lord will not cast off forever: But though he causes grief, yet will he have compassion according to the multitude of his mercies." (Lamentations 3:31-32)

I was sixteen the day my father died. It was February 8, 1998, and on that exact date and the exact moment my father took his last breath, for a period of my life, I became an orphan. I remember the moment it hit me that both of my parents were gone, one permanently from this earth, and one temporarily from "the world." On the day my father died, my mother, with whom my relationship was broken and shattered, was incarcerated. I'd already gone through the hurt of losing my mom to the system; but on the day my father died, I felt the void & loss of both of my parents.

There are moments in your life that you'll never forget. You will always be able to recall them as if you're watching a movie. The day my father died is one of those moments. My father died on a Sunday. This is significant because about an hour before he died, he became an ordained minister. There was a celebration for him at church, and I recall going upstairs to his room to tell him we were leaving. He had been in hospice care for several weeks, and I remember him standing up, trying to walk around his bed. I tried to coax him back into lying down, with him repeatedly saying to me "I'm ready."

At the moment, I didn't know what he meant. He knew. Our savior knew. On the day my father died, he waited until my grandmother, stepmother, baby sister and I were out of the house before taking his last breath. Although I miss him tremendously, I was blessed to have him for the time that I did. His work was done. I find joy & solace in knowing I've made him proud.

Dr. Angela Seay

"Ms. D3" is an Educator, published author, and entrepreneur. D3 Health & Fitness where we help individuals identify the missing variable(s) in their health-fit and wellness equation and offer solutions for a healthier lifestyle. https://www.d3healthfit.com IG D3HealthFitness FB D3 Health & Fitness.

Pressing Forward, Keep Moving "Procrastination is NOT your friend!" Dr. A. Seay

13 Brothers and sisters, I do not consider myself yet to have taken hold of it. But one thing I do: Forgetting what is behind and straining toward what is ahead, 14 I press on toward the goal to win the prize for which God has called me heavenward in Christ Jesus. (Philippians 3:13-14 NIV)

Life happens, and we experience loss. We lose loved ones, jobs, friendships, relationships, etc. We have no control over who, what, when why, or how. Everybody mourns in some form, shape, or fashion. However, what can be controlled is how we respond to the loss.

Here are a few options:

1. Cry a river, build a bridge, and get over it. Stay focused on your purpose.
2. Cry a river and become a victim of "Woe, it's me." Lose sight of your purpose and complain.

Choose 1. Losing sight of your purpose by focusing on the circumstances will keep you in a losing state. It is imperative to keep pressing forward, to keep working, to keep a positive mindset, and focus on your purpose, rather than highlight a temporary loss. Yes, it may hurt. It may be disappointing, but it is not the end. Think about it like this: Reflect and appreciate what you have learned from the experiences during the tenue, and continue to grow and glow. Always think positive and expect greater. You will be glad that you did! Start today. Decide to keep moving, and press forward, knowing that brighter days are ahead, and the best is yet to come.

Rev. Starsha Sewell

is a prophetic intercessor and social justice advocate; with a mandate to bring healing and deliverance to God's people. Rev. Sewell is a Subject-Matter Expert in Higher Academia Organizational Leadership Development & Training, using her spiritual gifts and talents to birth solutions to complex challenges onset by injustices.

Five Faith-Based Strategies to Overcome Loss Onset by Injustice

"For I will forgive their wickedness and will remember their sins no more."
(Hebrews 8:12 NIV)

Rev. Starsha M. Sewell, CSM, M.Ed., built a Cyber Security, Training & Disaster Recovery Company in response to a tragedy created by a Detective's non-compliance with State and Federal orders, issued by the Second Highest Court in the Nation to protect the civil rights of my minor children, who were ultimately displaced for several years and entrapped systematically by the incorrect court. The case gained national attention, and while painful, I coped with grief but fought back with the creation of my ministry dedicated to uncommon intercession and Prayer as a Weapon of War.

I am more than a biological mother to my children; I evolved as their Spiritual mother and entrusted God to care for them, and He did, while also taking care of me. Rather, than condemning the Detective for enforcing the incorrect orders,

I presented the correct orders to her leadership; and filed a criminal complaint to mitigate damages. Even if the situation is painful, please do not give up on God or the greater good of law enforcement in our Nation, because they are necessary.

Five faith-based Strategies to Overcome Loss Onset by Injustice

Forgive, Correct, Be Persistent, Endure & Trust God & Pray

These strategies helped me to acquire God's mentality in Hebrews 8:12 (NIV) *"For I will forgive their wickedness and will remember their sins no more."* I received a job offer with the Federal Bureau of Investigation, for capabilities that arose from this circumstance, proving that Joy comes in the morning.

Elaine Ezzell Shelley

is a mother, grandmother, and lover of just being you and being happy. Elaine retired from the Army after serving 20 years and holds a B.S. in Information Systems Technology and MBA in Acquisitions.

LOVE - TRUST - BELIEVE

"Trust in the Lord with all thine heart; and lean not unto thine own understanding. In all thy ways acknowledge him, and he shall direct thy paths."
(Proverbs 3:5-6)

Love, trust, belief sounds easy, right? However, for many of us, those things are hard to do. Oftentimes our difficulty comes not just in our perception of ourselves but also from the events we have experienced. For those of us who have suffered the loss of a loved one, one of the hardest things to do is not get stuck in grief. I've found myself in that sandpit of sadness after my husband died.

I was mad at him, myself, and yes even at God. I kept asking, God, how could you finally give me the man I've been praying for and take him away so suddenly. I mean what was the purpose of showing me happiness only to take it away? One day, while watching television, I heard Iyanla keep repeating "Lean not on your understanding," and that resonated with me to do something about my sadness.

I've always been an introvert and never allowed people to get too close, however, when God brought Ron into my life, it was as if, through Ron, I was being shown how to truly surrender and love God too. With Ron, I could just be me, and I believe that was God's way of showing me how to fully trust in the Lord and know that everything will be okay.

Life is not an easy journey but with God, we can be sure that he will get us through. Even during grief, you can find joy by doing something in memory of your loved one like joining a walking or hiking group. The key is to live life and not just exist in it. Peace, Love & Blessings.

Loretha Simon

Amazon International #1 Best Selling Author loves the Lord. She recently graduated from International Seminary, Plymouth, FL with an Advanced Diploma in Practical Theology II. Loretha evangelizes with The TOUR that Angie BEE Presents and with Child Evangelism Fellowships "Good News Club."
https://www.Facebook.com/Loretha.Simon
https://www.Facebook.com/Penofareadywriter Loretha.Simon844@gmail.com

Though I Mourn Their Passing, Just Thinking of Them Gives Me Joy, Which Comes from The Lord

"And not only so, but we also joy in God through our Lord Jesus Christ by whom we have now received the atonement." (Romans 5:11)

Loretha Q. Osby (King) is my Beloved Aunt and namesake. Affectionately known as "Lo-Lo" she was a vibrant soul – one who lit up the room whenever she entered. She had an inherent love of music and taught it for 43 years. Aunt Loretha was a preacher's kid and a student of James Cleveland, the King of the Gospel. She valued literacy, enjoyed traveling, and had a fondness for bridge. Yellow roses gave her so much joy.

Richard S. Quarterman, III was my only brother and he, too, was his father's namesake. He grew up to become a fine fellow who protected his four sisters. We often wondered whether we would ever have a date. My brother was very talented. His God-given gift was athleticism as he grew to become 6'8" tall and earned a full college scholarship. Richard's passion was basketball. He was a gentle giant who gave us joy. He loved the Lord, and I loved him. I am my brother's keeper.

Dr. Rebecca Walker Steel was married to John G. Steel for over 60 years. They were an adored, esteemed couple. Together they entertained Governors and our U.S. troops. She entertained with her prowess as a world-renowned concert choral music director and with her vocal performances. Dr. Steel's production of "From Bach to Gospel" is widely celebrated. Her beloved husband, John, was a Montford Point Marine and a recipient of a Congressional Gold Medal. John told great stories of when he and my dad were at FAMC. They both gave me joy.

Darlene Smith

is a mother, grandmother, professional chef, TV personality, culinary instructor, and author. I enjoy traveling to expand my knowledge in the culinary industry. I am a small business owner and I can be reached at chefdarlene.com where I sell organic and seasonal products.

CHEFFIN WITH JOY

"I can do all things through Christ who strengthens me."
(Philippians 4:13)

I've been strong my whole life, and the oldest memory I have was around three. I carried 2 gallons of paint up a flight of stairs. I often think of that when I'm struggling with issues.

Cooking for celebrities, winning gold medals, working in beautiful restaurants, hotels, resorts, being able to bring thoughts to life and create beautiful desserts was such a rewarding experience, but it wasn't always like that. When I first started cooking classes, I went through so much pain during this time. I was married and had three kids and one on the way. My husband was unsupportive of me becoming a chef even after I had won five gold medals, competed in various state competitions, and won a scholarship to go to culinary school. I struggled as a single parent to get my children to daycare before 6 am while going through a divorce

Let me tell you, it was all my faith in God and my very close friends during those difficult times knowing that God will strengthen my every step. I had to have faith and believe in myself to achieve my goals by praying and asking God to hold me because I wanted to complete school and become a chef.

The pains of life can destroy you if you allow them to; my strong faith and sense of self is what kept me going. I believe in this scripture: "I can do all things through Christ that strengthens me." People asked how did I manage to persevere through school, kids, and a divorce. I say my cooking instructor once said, "you have a winner's mentality. You only bring home gold." Never give up your goal! Keep joy and forgiveness in your heart. It's your life! You control the narrative. It reminds me of the church song "Joy." Keep the joy in your heart to stay. This is the way I choose to live my life. I live it with joy.

Takia Chase-Smith

is a Wife and Mother of three amazing children. She is a Veteran who specializes in Helping Youth. She can be found on social media FB, and IG as Author Takia Chase Smith
My website is www.authortakia.mystrikingly.com

JOY DURING TRIALS

"When I am filled with cares, your comfort brings me joy."
(Psalm 94:19 CSB)

Proverbs 10:28 (CSB): "The hope of the righteous is joy, but the expectation of the wicked will perish."

James 1:2-4 (CSB): "Consider it a great joy, my brothers and sisters, whenever you experience various trials, because you know that the testing of your faith produces endurance. And let endurance have its full effect, so that you may be mature and complete, lacking nothing."

During a challenging situation, it's difficult to see yourself as a diamond forming under pressure. The psalmist had many troubled thoughts concerning the circumstance he was in, the course he should take, and what was likely the end of it. When we fear, it adds worry and distrust, and our views are gloomier and more confused. Sometimes we have perplexed and distressed thoughts concerning God. Therefore, we must look to the great and precious promises of His Word. The world's comforts give little delight to the soul, but God's comforts bring that peace and pleasure that the world cannot give.

Jehovah Father, thank You for the life lessons I have learned from my darkest days and longest nights. Thank You for setting apart each of us to know You and for answering when I call to You. Let the smile of Your countenance shine on me this day. Grant me joy in Christ and peace in Your presence, even before a turnaround or harvest comes. And when the night falls, grant me to lie down in peace and sleep, for You alone keep me safe. Amen.

Valerie Stancill

"What I have been through, will help you get through..." is the mantra she lives by. After living through her trials and setbacks she knew her experiences were not only for her. She moves full steam ahead daily to fulfill her passion to educate, empower, inspire, and equip women to regain control of their life and wellness so they can live abundantly emotionally, mentally, and spiritually. After completing her studies in Health Arts at the University of St. Francis; she continued to hone her craft by becoming certified as a holistic wellness coach, licensed massage therapist, certified Yoni Steam practitioner, certified Reiki Master Practitioner, and certified Etheric Touch practitioner. To book or connect with Valerie, please use the links below:
Email: valerie@purposedforwellness.com :
https://www.facebook.com/PurposedForWellness
https://www.instagram.com/purposedforwellness/

JUST JOY

(Galatians 5:22-23)

We all look for ways to experience joy in our lives. Is it always a "joyful feeling?"

Is it something we have control over? Is there something that makes it hard to decipher what gives us our joy? Is it our family, job, or maybe our hobbies? Is that truly where our joy lives . . . where it comes from?

Joy is an emotion; it can be lived in different ways as we allow our spirits to understand "Joy."

The Spirit can create joy even in times filled with circumstances and then you can also experience the exuberance of joy from something pleasurable.

The enemy can make those same situations look devastating since he tries to make us think we always have to do something good to obtain it.

God did not make "Joy" out of our control. He made it to fit any circumstance because it is a reminder of Him and His love for us. He will remain the same and provide the necessary need in both good and bad times.

Sometimes we forget that we know who can provide our joy no matter the circumstance. His joy is consistent, and it's given daily AND freely. As you walk through your different journeys, learn how to make JOY your intentional choice.

Look for it in both the good and the bad, knowing He is there for both. Start planting those seeds of JOY, and take those steps to experience developing your relationship with God who will provide you with this fruit: The spirit of Joy.

Rosa Sylvester

is an actress, minister, mother of three, prayer intercessor, radio co-host, and much more. Rosa is from a small town near Elizabeth City, North Carolina, and resides on the south side of Atlanta, Georgia. Connect with her on Facebook and Instagram, Rosa Sylvester.

The Power of Thankfulness

"Rejoice always, pray continually, give thanks in all circumstances; for this is God's will for you in Christ Jesus." (I Thessalonians 5:16-18 NIV)

While going through trials and tribulations, it may be hard to give thanks; however, the Bible encourages us to give thanks in all situations. Shifting our focus to delight in the things that brings joy to our heart is key. It is helpful to remember the little blessings to give God thanks for. His love surrounds us every day.

Although the sun may not shine brightly sometimes, we can still thank God that we can see, breathe, taste, smell, and touch. There is something to always give God thanks for. Counting your blessings perse; forcing yourself to utter out loud what you are thankful for helps to reset your atmosphere and to give way for positive energy to enter the room. The more you elevate your thanks, the better you will feel.

Here's my story: I was crying and boo-hoo-ing about something that was going wrong in my life that was making me unhappy. I remembered God's word, "give thanks." Of course, I could not give thanks for my bad situation, but I gave Him thanks for my children being safe, for having a home to live in, and for the utilities being on because at one time I had nothing. I thanked God for my job because I was once jobless.

I rejoiced that the Lord was keeping me through all my hard times. I knew he was going to see me through little by little. I thanked him in advance for my victory. You can do the same.

GIVE THANKS!

Winona L. Thomas

is a Certified Professional Author Coach and is seen as one of Metropolitan Detroit's rare treasures. Known for her many accomplishments including Founder of Kira's Publishing LLC, talk & radio show host, author of five inspirational books, writer of inspirational poetry, prayers, reflections, and thematic plays.

Social Media:
Instagram: www.instagram.com/winona.thomas Facebook: www.facebook.com/winonalthomas LinkedIn: www.linkedin.com/in/winona-l-thomas Website: https://www.kiraspublishing.com
Book: https://linktr.ee/BeautifulYouInside Contact: 734.330.2140
Email: info@kiraspublishing.com

Refined for Resilience

"He has sent me to provide for all those who grieve in Zion, to give them crowns instead of ashes, the oil of joy instead of tears of grief, and clothes of praise instead of a spirit of weakness. They will be called Oaks of Righteousness, the Plantings of the Lord so that He might display His glory." (Isaiah 61:1-3 MSG)

If you check the Webster dictionary, to refine something means to be freed or free from; freed from impurities. Resilient means to return to the original form or position after being bent, compressed, or stretched. Resilient can also be defined as recovering readily from illness, depression, adversity.

When I received the devastating diagnosis of breast cancer, when I separated from my husband amid the cancer diagnosis, and when I lost my beloved grandmother, I was somewhere in unknown territory. For me, unknown territory meant not being sure of how I was going to make it back to my place of peace or if I was going to make it back at all. One of my favorite scriptures is Psalm 23 beginning at verse 4, "Yea though I walk through the valley of the shadow of death, I will fear no evil: for thou art with me; thy rod and thy staff they comfort me." As I was walking on this path of loss, sickness, and death, I found myself walking through the "valley of the shadow of death."

In my journey of healing, I realized that God was restoring me and transforming every aspect of who He had created me to be. When God takes us through and brings us out of the "valley of the shadow of death," He has refined us for resilience so that we can walk in His promise of long life.

Shaunda Thompson

is an Author, Facilitator, and Holistic Personal Development Coach. Ms. Thompson specializes in job search and networking strategy, interviewing, career and life transitions, personal branding, and image coaching. She is a connector and is passionate about connecting women to their healing and purpose.

Contact Info:
Website- www.shaundathompson.com Facebook- www.facebook.com/coachshaunda IG: @shaundathompson_official

Bent Not Broken

*"We are hard-pressed on every side, but not crushed.
Perplexed but not in despair, persecuted but not abandoned.
Struck down but not destroyed." (2 Cor. 4:8)*

I've never been good at saying goodbye. Today was no exception. Every fiber of my being shook in disbelief as I watched The Respiratory Technician turn off the ventilator and remove the breathing tube from the fragile body of my premature baby boy. Suddenly the room was quiet. A few minutes ago, the beeping of all the machines was a beacon of hope. Now, the silence was deafening. I felt despair settle in the pit of my stomach. As I cradled my son in my arms, I matched his shallow breathing with mine. I didn't want to miss his last breath. As I slowly and gently rocked him back and forth, I lovingly bestowed kisses on his tiny forehead and nose. A sudden intake of breath and then a soft wail. My beloved Brock was gone. Grief and sadness clotted the air. Within 24 hours, Brock took a turn for the worst and went from thriving to dying.

Time is precious and not to be wasted.

For an object to bend, it requires force to direct or turn it in a particular direction. Losing my son was the force that ignited a fire inside of me to take back my life. I said YES to self-love. I said YES to ending an abusive and toxic marriage. I said YES to healing by doing the work and understanding the pathology of my dysfunction in relationships. I said YES to trusting and finding love again. What are you ready to say YES to? We are all living on borrowed time. How are you using it? Are you thriving or dying? Seek God. Sit at his feet daily. Be intentional with your decisions. You can keep moving forward despite your circumstances when you have clarity and peace of mind.

Erica D. Tobias

is a Greenwood, Mississippi native, currently residing in Brandon, Mississippi. She is a Program Assistant in the Upward Bound I Program, a published author, and a Godly proud member of the Theta Chapter of Alpha Eta Theta Christian Sorority, Inc.

Seasons Change

"To everything, there is a season and a time to every purpose under the heaven:"
(Ecclesiastes 3:1)

The season is defined as a suitable, proper, fitting time. Change is defined as transforming or converting. Every season we face in life brings about a change; nothing stays the same. But, just like the seasons in nature change, the third chapter of Ecclesiastes reminds us that life's seasons change.

The season we are currently in has caused a lot of change. We went from being able to be outside, being with friends and family, shopping, dining freely, without wearing a mask to having to isolate, be vaccinated, be quarantined, and wear masks. This pandemic season is considered the "new norm". But, even in this, seasons change.

This season, for some, has caused sickness, death, job loss, loss of income, poverty, and famine. This season has caused loss of faith, hurt, worry, fear and doubt. Simply put, this, for some, is a season of chaos.

On the flip side of the chaos of this pandemic season, some have gotten closer to God through fasting, prayer, reading, and studying the Word of God. Some have flourished financially. Some have started thriving businesses. For some, this has been the right time to step out on faith.

If you are in your season of lack, be encouraged and stand firm in the knowledge that you won't be there long; it is only a season. I'm reminded of a line in the song, "Seasons" by Donald Lawrence, that states: "you survived the worst of times, God was always on your side." Just look to God and trust Him. Don't worry and don't fret. Just remember, child of God, seasons change.

Shanta' Tobias

is a Jackson, Ms. native, currently residing in the Houston, Tx area. She is a Dialysis Technician, a Licensed Insurance Agent/adjuster, and a licensed eyelash e tension Technician. She is also an entrepreneur with Tori Belle Cosmetics.

There Is Still Purpose to Fulfill

"For Scripture says to Pharaoh: "I raised you for this very purpose, that I might display my power in you and that my name might be proclaimed in all the earth." (Romans 9:17 NIV) https://romans.bible/romans-9-17

Many of us have suffered the loss of some of the people and possessions that we valued the most. With these losses, we struggled to keep our peace. The faith that we once held so strongly became shaken. It felt as if hope was lost. Our mental, emotional, and spiritual health took devastating blows causing us to lose focus and lose sight of our divine purpose. Some of us have gone from living to just existing.

There is still breath in our bodies and warm blood flowing through our veins which means we still have a purpose to fulfill. What is the purpose? The purpose is the reason for our existence. Why are we here? We are here to fulfill the very reason of our being. How do we find purpose? Pay close attention to what brings joy, peace, a sense of warmth, what we are passionate about. Know that God impregnated us with purpose, therefore we must give birth to that thing. How can we get back on track? We must first identify the root cause of what affected our focus. Then we have to take ALL of our: frustrations, concerns, hurts, and fears, to God in prayer. Psalms 55:22, Holy Bible NIV, reads, "cast your cares on the Lord and he will sustain you; he will never let the righteous be shaken."

When we go before the Lord in spirit and truth he will hear our cries, he will answer us, and he will instruct us. We just have to be open to and accept HIS will and his way. We must obey and trust him. God may isolate us to regroup, recharge, prepare and groom us for a season, and it's ok! Also, keep in mind purpose may not be what WE think it is, but it must be fulfilled.

Tamron Tobias

from Metairie, La. Author, Entrepreneur with Tori Bell Cosmetics, Filmmaker & Entertainment Journalist, & Caregiver.
A graduate of Jackson State University, B.S. Mass Communications, Savannah College of Art & Design (ATL), M.F.A. Television & Film, Hinds Community College, A.A. Radio, Television, and Film.

I Am God's Thoughts

*"For I know the thoughts that I think toward you, saith the Lord, thoughts of peace, and not of evil, to give you an expected **end**." (Jeremiah 29:11)*

We've heard the saying "Life is what you make it. Live it to the fullest, and don't let people tell you how to live it." Yet we still allow people to tell us how to live our lives, sometimes to the point that we are confused about what we want for our own lives.

Do you remember as a child wanting to be a Policeman, Firemen, Doctor, Lawyer, Teacher, etc., and as you grew older either that dream stayed with you or you took on other interest (s)? Although your family and friends wanted you to be who they wanted you to be, God's thoughts and plans for your life have never changed.

He gave you certain gifts and talents for a reason. You may be a Hairstylist, Barber, MUA, Fashionista because he knew someone needed to know Psalms 139:14 *"I will praise thee; for I am fearfully and wonderfully made: marvelous are thy works; and my soul knoweth right well."*

You may be a Teacher, Counselor, or Pastor because he knew his people would need to be reminded of II Timothy 2:15 *"Study to shew thyself approved unto God, a workman that needeth not to be ashamed, rightly dividing the word of truth."* As my teachers and Pastor would always teach me, "show your work so that I know you understand what was being taught."

So, you see, God's thoughts towards you were always pure, but he had to take us through life's major intersections and stand-still traffic zones to get us to where we are now.

Just remember and declare with boldness: "I AM GOD'S THOUGHTS".

Arlene Townsend

is a Pastor, published author, and radio host. Connect with her at:
<u>Arlenetownsend96@gmail.com</u>

Your Joy Is Coming

"I lift my eyes to the mountains where does my help come from? My help comes from the Lord, the Maker of heaven and earth." (Psalm 121:1-2 NIV)

After the death of two of my sons to a devastating rare blood disease, a woman asked me "how could you possibly keep your faith? How could you still say you love God?" I thought about it for a few minutes and replied, "God is the love of my life. Just because my sons are dead that does not mean that I would stop loving him. He is the strength and source of everything that I am."

I remember the day that I asked the Lord to take me into his kingdom. I was a mess. I felt like I had done so much and gone too far in this life, and he did not let me down. He took me, cleaned me up, and allowed a person like me to pastor his people. He is the only one that has given me unconditional love.

He was the only one that believed in me. When I read the above scripture, I can hardly believe now that I can look to the one that has made everything and call him my father. That is where my joy comes from. The maker and creator of heaven and earth took time to love me when I did not love myself.

I pray that God will fill you from the top of your head to the soles of your feet with more joy than you have ever had before. Find your joy today in his love.

Ray'Chel Wilson

based in Black Wall Street, Tulsa, OK, is a former teacher, financial literacy speaker, 3 published author & entrepreneurship advocate. Below, she shares her experience as a "preacher's kid" and losing her father. Connect with her on LinkedIn at Ray'Chel Wilson or on her business website www.RTBinvestments.org.

A DEVOTIONAL FOR DADDY'S GIRLS

"Now to Him who can do exceedingly abundantly above all that we ask or think, according to the power that works in us," (Ephesians 3:20 NKJV)

We don't need to hear how hard it is to lose a father or father figure - we know. At the end of my freshman year of high school, I lost my dad to a heart attack. He was my biggest support system, and all I knew was that my rock was gone. What I needed at that moment was peace & I spent years trying to create it myself. Sound familiar? I wish I would have known that the more I incorporated God into my grief journey, the more I would know what peace felt like again.

We can heal, alone. We can exist alone, too. However, we are called to do more than exist, more than survive, but to thrive. We can only heal & thrive through faith. Do you have faith that the chair you're sitting in will continue to hold up? Or the building you're in or near will stay stable? If so, who are we to limit the power of God to heal within us, transform the missing parts in our hearts, remove the negative thoughts in our minds, and bring courage to our spirits? Think about what that could feel like for you. He can heal us abundantly. Are you ready?

Have the faith to affirm yourself in these affirmations daily, knowing that God will renew your heart, mind, and spirit:

- I know peace because God is peace.
- I have courage because Christ had courage.
- I attract healing friendships in alignment with my purpose.
- I am creative through the power of the Holy Spirit within me.
- I walk in abundance as a daughter of Christ.

Interventions are blocking God's plan for your life? Do you trust God through the pain?

Verlisa Wearing

is the mother of three, USMC Veteran, Ordained Minister, Speaker, Transition Empowerment Coach, 2x Best-selling Author and CEO/Owner of It Is Written Publishing, LLC.
It is her goal to assist 1,000 women to build their confidence and see their worth in order to make their dream into reality.
www.verlisawearing.com

Arise and Shine

"Arise, shine, for your light has come, and the glory of the Lord rises upon you."
(Isaiah 60:1 NIV)

Each morning you awaken is a gift given from our Heavenly Father. For the believer of Christ, these words not only hold a special place in our lives but, ensure that no matter what, God is with us.

Despite the chaos, frustrations and disappointments that may show up in life, our day and lives are encompassed by the light and favor of Jesus Christ.

For many, the day may begin unsettling for reasons of health, angry bosses and complaining associates. But still, we rise. When rising each morning, each day, every minute of the day are you being intentional in allowing your light to shine, even with the things that do not make you feel satisfied, uplifted or even empowered? We must be grateful for these moments as they are opportunities for the glory of the Lord to be shown through us.

Whatever you may be dealing with on today, remember the Lord is with you and his glory is upon you. This thought will allow His glory to rise.

Today's Prayer:

Lord Jesus, I thank you for being the light that shines within me. Continue to remind me, you will never leave nor forsake me. In the darkness that surrounds, Father, allow me to feel your glory rising up within me. Today I turn my face, my thoughts and my actions to you. I thank you that on this day, I receive brand new mercies you have towards me. Thank you for gracing me. Now I can show grace unto another.

Dr. Jenaya White

*is a social entrepreneur, motivational speaker, author, and award-winning community leader with a passion for helping girls and women become the best versions of themselves through her empowerment organization.
Connect with her by visiting www.jenayawhite.com
You may also connect with her on all social media platforms with the social media handle: @jenayawhite*

The Promise of Restoration

"Arise, shine, for your light has come, and the glory of the Lord rises upon you"
(Isaiah 60:1)

You are now entering a season of new beginnings and abundance. God is going to take your tears of sorrow and turn them into tears of joy. God never intended for you to accept defeat because He is a God of restoration.

When God restores, He does not take you back to the place you were before you experienced brokenness. God's restoration plans always consist of restoring things to you better than you could ever imagine. He is putting your life back in order and elevating you to excellence and greatness. Going through challenging times can be overwhelming and discouraging, However, God has given you the power to arise and shine.

God would not require you to do what He considers impossible. He knows your strength and what you ought to do at every phase of life. God wants you to have faith in Him without questioning, even if it looks impossible. Will you listen to His voice today when He tells you to arise and shine, or will you listen to the noise of situations around you, telling you to stay low?

When you put your trust in Him, God gives you rest, and you will rise above your problems. He will renew your strength and empower you to soar above your mountains and you will have the victory.

Difficult times will surely come, but God has promised you that yours will last only for a moment. You will quickly forget your days of suffering because God is about to do a new thing in your life. God is not only healing you; He is preparing you to be a source of healing and encouragement to others. Always remember, it is always darkest just before the day dawns. Therefore, your joy is about to burst forth just as the sunrises.

Stephanie White

Authoress SWD~ motto: a strong believer of faith and perseverance always allows her to overcome. A best- selling authoress, family-oriented, a mentor, inspirational coach, podcast "What's the Scoop Steph" https://linktr.ee/authoress_swd, https://authoress- swd.creator-spring.com, www.authoressswd.com

CLOUDS ...FAITH ...DECISIONS

Different images are often shown when looking at the clouds above us. Plenty of times, I'm sure not only myself have become amazed by the findings of what we see. We realize it wasn't an illusion, especially when others see with their own eyes.

What are the possibilities in having a leap of faith to step off a plane in the sky to place feet on pillars of clouds? Will you accept faith, responsibility, and a justified reason for doing it?

Imagine, stepping off a plane without a parachute. Prepare for the future and the outcome by choice, especially if it's not what you wanted it to be.

The reality of this tells us that without safety gear or an attachment to the plane, you can quickly impact concrete or an ocean when landing. In order to defeat the odds in the options you have been given, you want to make wise choices, especially if you know the results already stretch out for better opportunities. We have to own up to our own decisions within our mindset. Keep your faith and overcome your fears.

Malcolm Winder

is a Husband, Father, Grandfather, Uncle, and Disabled Retired Army Veteran with an MBA. His hometown is Charles County, MD. This is his first writing as a co- author in a collaboration with number one bestselling authors. His passion, love, and desire is mentoring/coaching through God's words and promises.

FORGIVING WHAT YOU CAN'T FORGET

"The Spirit of the Lord God is with me; because the Lord hath anointed me to preach good tidings unto the meek; he hath sent me to bind up the brokenhearted, to proclaim liberty to the captives, and the opening of the prison to them that are bound" (Isaiah 61:1)

Who said that life will be easy and that we will be able to go without struggle or pain? Have we learned to have faith and let God in all of our situations? Relax and know that God is always there with us. Fixing our heart, mind, and body is something a doctor may be able to do, but fixing our Soul is the work of God through us. The true fixing overall comes only from God, prayer, and our acceptance of Him.

Trials and tribulations are certain to come and will we deal with them accordingly or just wing it as some do? We are all human and deal with many things differently depending upon the situation and our feelings. The process of how we forgive and not forget is very detrimental in our lives.

Not an easy process, "Forgiving!" This should be the first action that tends to release us from carrying burdens, anger, hurt, maybe guilt, and or the person or thing that caused it all. Overall Forgiving keeps us from having a revengeful heart. Forgiveness takes our spirit into a better place of being and feeling better. Release yourself from captivity now by forgiving and praying for a way to forget also.

Forgetting is not the best sometimes because it can protect us possibly from the same unwanted situation happening again or to avoid the person, place, or thing. Of course, we do not want to forget the good times. We must give it to God in prayer that whatever it may be, God surely will and is working it out.

How did he survive twenty years plus feeling often hurt, angry, and managed to retire? Only by God's grace and mercy with having forgiveness and not forgetting!

Dr. Angela Basden-Williams

is a Financial/Life Insurance Agent, No.1 Best-selling Co- Author "Finding Joy in The Journey", College Consultant, Speaker, and Retired Correctional Lieutenant who worked 30+years in Corporate America.

Website: https://wsbcampaign.com/angelabasdenwilliams
Email: https://authorangela.mystrikingly.com Email: Angelaabwfg@gmail.com

KEEP SHINING BRIGHT LIKE A DIAMOND

"The Lord Bless you and keep you; The Lord make His face shine upon you and be gracious to you; The Lord lifts up His countenance upon you and gives you peace." (Number 6:24- 26)

Our life is created before the foundation of the world; we have the privilege and freedom to make choices. Sometimes, we may think we are making good decisions based upon our emotions, feelings, knowledge, and/or others' opinions. We pray that we are a good character of judgment about the people entering our life to love, assist and trust. My choices were always to be careful, compassionate, trustworthy, live a stressless and drama-free lifestyle with solid confidence, strength, and high self-esteem developed. When that falters, the errors of life create disappointments, distractions, tests, hurt, jealousy, pain, and rejection arise. It attempts to invade those desires for peace, serenity, mindset when you're determined to step out on Faith, embrace change further to conquer other dreams and/or visions.

This happens in business, family, friendships, workplace, partners, and in marriages; but the eyes of the Lord are everywhere keeping watch on the evil and the good. Life lessons build character, growth, patience, understanding yourself better, improving weakness, and the realization that we cannot control everything that happens. Leaders are not born but developed. Remember to preserve in your mind pass confusion and pressure. Do not be hard on yourself but practice positive self-talk and surround yourself with like-minded people. Our testimonies belong to God and it is not only for us. Our story is for encouragement, inspiration, helping others overcome this rigorous process, and start shining an illuminating like a diamond. Courage, strength, and success arise from adversity, trials, and tribulations when you do not surrender. God is the masterpiece and creator of us, He is the Author and Finisher of our Faith. God has provided us to win with Words of Wisdom, scriptures, parables, and biblical principles for finding joy in the mornings. It is a gift from Our Father.

Yonder

the Author. He has a total of nine books, including Murder Mystery, Poetry, Erotic and a Devotional

Who Am I? Why Am I Here?

"Do not forget to show hospitality to strangers, for by so doing some people have shown hospitality to angels without knowing it." (Hebrews 13:2)

Who am I and why am I here?

Some days I don't know, and some days I do.

When I was younger, I was just searching for something. I got a little older, and the search became vast and slow. I needed more knowledge, so I prayed. I needed new skills, so I studied. I needed more influence, so I hung with a new crew as I searched for my place in life to find myself. As I found myself, I realized I already had Jesus in my heart.

My heart grew bigger, and my style and ego followed as I matured. As time continued to move, so did I. Once I loved others and helped others, it all came together.

I felt good about just being myself. With God on my side, nothing could stop me as I am all I need to be in this life. Along the way, life just got better and better and I realized I needed to be kind to myself, so, along the way, I loved me even more despite the fact that there was still some pain and even some family deaths.

So, you can enjoy me, and I hope you enjoy yourself. May the Lord have patience with you as he did with me.

www.ingramcontent.com/pod-product-compliance
Lightning Source LLC
Chambersburg PA
CBHW071920290426
44110CB00013B/1426